Faith and Hungry Grass

A MAYO BOOK OF THEOLOGY

Edited by

Enda McDonagh

the columba press

THE COLUMBA PRESS
93 The Rise, Mount Merrion, Blackrock, Co Dublin, Ireland

First edition 1990
Cover by Bill Bolger
Origination by The Columba Press
Printed in Ireland by
Betaprint Ltd, Dublin

ISBN: 0 948183 88 8

The Editor and publishers acknowledge the permission of the following to use material in their copyright: Oxford University Press for the quote from *Ecce Homo* by David Gascoyne; Thomas Kinsella for his translations used in the chapter *A Passionate God?*

Copyright © 1990, The Columba Press and The Contributors

Contents

Preface: *Archbishop Joseph Cassidy*   5

Introduction: Between Westport and Asia Minor   7
Enda McDonagh

PART I: FAITH IN PLACE

1   Land and Gospel   17
    Seán Freyne
2   Faith and Fear: The Christian Disciple   27
    Michael Neary
3   Sacrament of God   35
    Enda Lyons
4   Woman of Faith   44
    Augustine Valkenburg
5   A Lost Tradition?   54
    Leon Ó Mórcháin

PART II: EXILES AND PILGRIMS

6   Exile and Return   66
    Donal Dorr
7   Faith: A Pilgrim Condition   82
    Mary Guy
8   God in Ordinarie   89
    Brendan Hoban
9   Power or Empowerment? – A Woman's Perspective   101
    Ben Kimmerling
10   Inferiority or Good News?   114
    Ned Crosby
11   Liturgy for Exiles   122
    Thomas Waldron

PART III: ATLANTIC GOD

12   Journey from Achill   134
    John F. Deane
13   Cassandra: Island in Mayo   146
    Patrick O Brien
14   Forever on the Periphery   157
    Pádraig Standún
15   A Passionate God?   163
    Enda McDonagh

The Contributors   175

Preface

The Balla farmer's remark, in the seventies, that 'farming is gone to the dogs, but agriculture is thriving' was adapted by a clerical commentator to 'religion is gone to the dogs, but theology is thriving.'

Too smart, of course. Neither part is really true, at least not in the West of Ireland. There is still a great deal of vital Christian faith and practice. Religion survives, even thrives in many ways. There is, no doubt, more reading and discussion by clergy and, especially, laity than there used to be. There is a range of part-time courses.

Yet as the secular challenges to an intelligent and systematic understanding of the faith grow, the response is very limited. The most obvious single lack is some institutional presence of theology in the western half of Ireland. Indeed if one takes a line from Newry to Cork, there is not a single Catholic centre for theology north or west or south-west of that line. That means no serious theological library in three quarters of the country. No regular centre for theology conferences; no place where people can go to read and write theology.

It is all the more surprising and exciting therefore to find fifteen people from Mayo contributing to a Mayo book of theology. And a distinctive theology it proves: with the history and geography, the languages and images, the wealth and poverty of Mayo interacting fruitfully with the Christian faith-tradition. Such an experiment must encourage a reflective and committed Irish church, the only kind of church which will survive into the new history and geography, the twenty-first century and a united Europe.

By drawing on the personal and communal faith resources of Mayo, this book offers a new way of Christian self-understanding, a new way of doing theology. The risks are obvious. The mistakes will emerge. Yet *Faith and the Hungry Grass* will surely contribute to the thriving of both religion and theology in Mayo and in Ireland.

Guím rath Dé ar an obair.

✠ *Joseph Cassidy*
Archbishop of Tuam

To the memory of
J. G. McGarry
Mayoman, Pastor and Theologian

Introduction:
Between Westport and Asia Minor

Enda McDonagh

Bleak and beautiful. To many people Mayo appears like that. Certainly to many Mayo people. And too many Mayo people remember it like that. Remembering is what they are good at. It is all they have of Mayo. Both the bleakness and the beauty are misleading, misremembering even. There was and is so much softness and so much warmth in so many features of the landscape. There is much ugliness too and not just in the cutaway bogs but in the harshness of life and in its inevitable impact on the people. Mayo is not for romanticising and it does not normally produce romantics. There may be a poetry in the speech, as Synge and others recognised, but there is the living which precludes romanticism.

Besides Mayo is not all that different. County boundaries are artificial, fostered in recent times by the rise of the GAA. Mayo merges with Sligo, Roscommon and Galway across elusive borders and through a shared history and lifestyle. 'To Hell or to Connacht' did not make any sharp trans-Shannon distinctions. Now Connacht belongs not only to Ireland but to Western and Greater Europe, and to an increasingly unified planet. Westport has developing links with Asia Minor as some long-distance lorry-drivers could attest. The tachograph seals the covenant, of commerce at least.

A Mayo book of theology, then, needs considerable explanation and justification. One world and one Christian faith suggest one faith-exploration or theology. Indeed, a Mayo theology book appears regressive in these ecumenical and uniting nations' days. It is in the theological trade unusual and perhaps unique. Its justification lies partly in its origins and partly in the localisation of theology, and of other intellectual enterprises, as counter-balance to the rush to universalisation in commerce, of course, but also in politics and in culture. Religion, and its intellectual assistant theology, can never disengage from the currents and counter-currents of their contemporary world. At least Christian faith cannot disengage and remain true to its creation and incarnation origins and to its missionary mandate. In the last few decades, particularly since the Vatican Council, the local community of the Catholic Church has become more significant. This was expressed in a number of ways by emphasising bishops' conferences, by development of priests' councils, by synods and other assemblies of the laity. The best known of these developments occurred in Latin America with their Basic Christian Communities at the immediately local level and the Latin-American Bishops' conference (CELAM) at continental level. Their meetings at Medellin in 1968 and at Puebla in 1979 have become bench marks in the development of local churches and of local theologies. Latin American Liberation Theology, which developed out of the basic communities and was endorsed and promoted by the meetings of the Bishops' conference, has become the most influential form of Catholic and, indeed, of Christian theology today. It is not without its critics, including some at the Vatican. However, as a theology emerging out of a particular context and out of a particular geographical region, admittedly on a grand scale, it has restored to theology its original sense of place and time.

Theology is not the faith. It is an attempt to interpret and understand the faith in the world of its day. So did Paul and Augustine and Aquinas and the great contemporary Europeans like Karl Rahner and Yves Congar. Because European thought and culture were for so long dominant in the world, through European and then North American power, the need for particular theologies had been obscured by the apparent success of imperial European theology, whether of a Roman or German kind. Local believing communities must now seek to understand the one Christian faith in the particularities of their own time and place.

All this must seem excessive in justification of a Mayo theology. Mayo's population of 115 thousand hardly rates beside Latin America's 400 million. The teeming diversity of people, states and cultures of the huge continent could make any Mayo claims to fertile interchange between faith and place ridiculous. That may be to miss the point, even the Latin American point about the importance of local reflection on the faith and the origins of all that in small local basic communities. For all its limitations of scale, Mayo may justly provide a context for faith exploration, if it can provide the explorers, the theologians.

The Mayo Theologians
All the contributors to this book were born and educated in Mayo. Many of them still live there. All of them had been engaged at some level in the theological enterprise, before being invited to reflect on the faith as Mayo people. It was their theological activities which prompted this book and not the book which drew them first into publishing on issues of faith. The project was really prompted by the story of one of us going into a newsagency in Ballyhaunis to buy his morning paper. The attendant whom he did not know said: 'I know who you are: you're the third best theologian in Mayo.' If not quite a Willie Joe Padden level of recognition, it did reveal an unexpected popular awareness of the species, theologian, and its relatively frequent occurrence in Mayo.

Mayoness is not all, even in theologians. The diversity of background, interest, activity and attitude of the fifteen contributors emerges clearly in this book. This background may lack the continental scope of central Europe or Latin America and their theologians, yet the diversity and the depth of the probings explore anew elements of that universal faith so scandalously founded in the particular villager we call Jesus the Christ.

> *Title and Structure*
> Crossing the shallow holdings high above the sea
> Where few birds nest, the luckless foot may pass
> From the bright safety of experience
> Into the terrors of the hungry grass.
> Donagh MacDonagh: *The Hungry Grass*

Féar Gorta, or hungry grass, was a feature of Mayo boyhood by which one could be stricken with inexplicable and excruciating hunger pains on stepping over a particular patch of ground. According to MacDonagh's poem and local tradition, someone had died or been buried here during the great famine in 1847. Mayo is deeply marked by that and later famines. The famine graves, for long neglected and even unknown, are now beginning to receive some overdue attention. Hungry grass brings together the tragic history and geography of Mayo. It has not all been tragic. Mayo is as happy as most areas in the country for all its past sufferings and current limitations. Related to that happiness and to the resilience of spirit which has characterised Mayo people at various stages, has been their Christian faith.

There is no simply Christian people. Mayo had and has its own share of pre-Christians and post-Christians. Most believing and practising Christians have their unbelieving and non-practising sides. Mayo Christians share in all these ambiguities. The Kindgom of God is not yet, certainly not in Mayo. The key interaction between Mayo history and geography and the Christian tradition, the key to a particular theology which might be tentatively described as Mayo theology, seemed well expressed in the phrase, *Faith and Hungry Grass*.

Structure followed more freely. When the potential participants had been identified and invited, an outline was suggested. Amendments were accepted. The actual contributions required further adjustment. So the structure emerges as somewhat contrived. Yet the three basic sections do offer an important move from the foundations of theology in scripture and doctrine, through the community context of church, to the ultimate confrontation with God in a story and an idiom which are redolent and resonant of Mayo people, place and story. *Faith in Place, Exiles and Pilgrims* and *Atlantic God* maintain connection between the major themes and the individual chapters of this book.

Faith in Place

'I don't know where he is coming from,' was a comment liable to be heard in the most exalted academic circles in years past. Not entirely mischievously I developed for my own inquisitors the simple answer, 'Mayo'. Mayo is where this book and its authors are coming from, not only geographically of course but culturally, socially, politically and religiously. Some of them may have come a long time ago but they were shaped by their early years there. They return regularly. They bear those secret mental tatoos which even they may only occasionally notice: 'It's the Mass that matters', and 'Mayo are magic' (very occasionally). Faith involves a dynamic combination of recognition, trust and engagement both as a moral phenomenon and as a religious one. Its immediate basis is laid in childhood, even if its adult specification may greatly change. Recognition, trust, and engagement with the world of place and people, form a continuing if changing life-task. That life-task may or may not continue to have an explicit religious dimension. But if it is truly life, it will still include the responses to reality of recognition, trust and engagement, responses of faith, however non-religious they may become. For us that life task began with the people and places of Mayo. In different ways and in varying degrees, it has retained its religious dimension as well as its Mayo character.

In biblical terms the localisation of faith, as several contributors note, is essential. While the God of Israel and of Jesus is beyond all doubt a universal God for all peoples, the divine strategy of working through particular places and peoples and their history, emphasises the presence of the universal in the particular, of the Creator in concretely created, and of the transcendent Other of God in the finite human other of the neighbour. Faith in place reflects that first encounter with the divine in the boglands of Bekan, and the cosmic context in which it must be pursued. The pursuit embodies the living circle of human lives.

> We shall not cease from exploration
> And the end of all our exploring
> Will be to arrive where we started
> And know the place for the first time.
>
> *T.S.Eliot: Little Gidding*

Exiles and Pilgrims

> On the deck of Patrick Lynch's boat I sat in woeful plight,
> Through my sighing all the weary day and weeping all the night
> Were it not that full of sorrow from my people forth I go
> By the blessed sun, 'tis royally I'd sing thy praise, Mayo.
>
> *The County of Mayo* (Version: *George Fox*)

Exile is so much part of the Mayo story that one writer here sees it as characteristic not only of the people who leave Mayo, but also of those who stay, exiles in their own country. This tragic history was often reinforced by a faith or spirituality which emphasised our human condition as strangers far from our true homeland in paradise. The 'poor banished children of Eve' exiled in this 'vale of tears' seemed an apt description for Mayo people en route from Foxford to Buenos Aires. The more sophisticated faith, like that of John Henry Newman which could see 'grace as glory in exile and glory as grace at home', was also part of Mayo schooling. The extremes of self-indulgent sentimentality and harsh cynicism yielded to a more realistic assessment of the joys and sorrows of the Mayo condition, human and Christian. The blind poet, Raifteirí (1779-1835) could not have been the first Mayo exile to look forward to the pilgrimage home. But he captured it for all Mayo people in the opening lines of his poem, *Cill Liadáin*:

> Tiocfaidh an t-earrach is beidh an lá ag síneadh
> Tar éis na Feil' Bríde ardód mo sheol
> Is ó chuir mé i mo cheann é ní chónóidh mé choíche
> Go seasfaidh mé thíos i lár Chontae Mhaigh Eo.

And in Brendan Kennelly's recent version:

> Now with the springtime there's a great stretch in the days
> And after Brigid's feastday I'll gather my traps and go,
> Since I took into my head, no chance that I'll delay
> Till I find myself in the middle of the County Mayo.

Life was a journey, often a physical as well as a human one, if you were from Mayo. Journey and pilgrimage, classic ways of Christian life, fitted the Mayo experience more neatly than most. Pilgrimage in the more religious sense was old and hallowed. It reached pre-Christian times with the sacred mountain now known as Croagh Patrick or, more affectionately, as The Reek. It had modern and famine resonances with Knock and the apparition of Mary in 1879. And to Knock came the pilgrim pope, John Paul II in 1979.

Anthropologist Victor Turner, specialist in pilgrimages, Hindu and Muslim as well as Christian, included The Reek and Knock in his classic study. His insight into Christian pilgrimage as breaking with the regular process of living to find fresh understanding of motivation, and as conversion to the deeper reaches of the Christian way, brings together the great themes of exile and pilgrimage. Estrangement from the already is the first step on the way to the not-yet – the Kingdom of God which is come and is yet to come in faith and sacrament, in community-building and ordinary living, in journey and in vision. Mayo exiles and pilgrims look to the transforming of their world in the promise of a wider Kingdom. Meantime, they encourage one another on the way with the stories and songs of the generations gone before them. Not all so sophisticated as Newman's *Lead Kindly Light* but with the more robust pub-sound of:

> Now boys pull together in all kinds of weather
> Like the stout-hearted men from the County Mayo.

Atlantic God

Mayo theology, like the Mayo story, is dominated by the Atlantic Ocean. Atlantic breakers from Killary Harbour to Killala Bay define and confine a restless people. At the same time they raise their eyes to other blessed and prosperous lands in Boston and Hybrasil. As barrier and bearer, the Atlantic shapes Mayo sensibility, religious and secular. Ultimate as well as economic questions take form in the sound and swell of that passionate sea. *Atlantic God* offers a fitting symbol for the final section of this book as the hungry land of Mayo and its land-hungry people face those boundary questions of human living and dying. In startlingly different ways, the authors here take their bearings from the Atlantic and its islands. Their perilous journeys carry them towards a God, passionate like the sea, which at once discloses and conceals him.

Atlantic God has the power and unpredictability of the God of Exodus 3:14, 'I will be who I will be.' This is no domestic idol, captive to the vanities and needs of a selfish and fearful people. Projections of human aspirations shatter on the rocks of the real God, creator and Lord of the ocean. Western reality principles have never allowed Celtic twilightery to obscure the harshness and the beauty of Mayo sea and landscape. In and through and beyond that harshness and beauty, Mayo faith discerns the creative and transforming God. It is the God of Creation who on the fifth day saw Mayo and that it was very good (Gen 1). It is the same God of Calvary crying in need, 'I thirst.' Such a God must understand the cry of Synge's Maura and of all Atlantic mothers:

> They're all together this time, and the end is come. May the Almighty God have mercy on Bartley's soul, and on Michael's soul, and on the souls of Sheamus and Patch and Stephen and Shawn, and may He have mercy on my soul, Nora and on the soul of every one who is left living in the world. Michael has a clean burial in the far north by the grace of Almighty God. Bartley will have a fine coffin out of the white boards, and a deep grave surely. What more can we want than that? No man at all can be living forever, and we must be satisfied..
>
> *Riders to the Sea*

Theology as Participatory

Fielding a team of fifteen theologians from the one county must seem over-ambitious to many who regard theology as a particularly elitist game. In its move from the universal to the local, theology is not abandoning the professional scholars. It is relativising them. As an exploration of the Christian life, theology must be more widely representative than any university or seminary could hope to be. It must be representative of the church as a whole, both the local eucharistic community and world-wide church. Scholars contribute essentially to theology. They do not finally determine it. For that, much broader participation is needed. Such participation has been the aim of this book. Of course, the contributors were chosen on their previous work in seeking to make sense of Christian faith, or to make loving sense of life, two broad but acceptable definitions of theology.

A team of scholars and pastors, of women and men with shared faith, origins and traditions, has been trying to offer their contemporaries more a model of how faith seeks understanding than some particularly new understanding of faith. That may be the main value of this book, some encouragement and instruction of other people and other teams as they seek faith understanding. The best confirmation of the work would be similar works from other teams, even another Mayo team. It might well happen.

O Westport in the Light of Asia Minor

Paul Durcan, whose line I stole, belongs to the larger Mayo. As I noted earlier, between Westport and Asia Minor there are geographical and historical bonds binding their peoples' traditions together. Mayo's village voices often concealed universal minds and sympathies. That other Paul's missionary journeys were our first exposure to Asia Minor. The exposure has lasted. No human place is alien to Mayo. Faith accounts for much of that universal sympathy. So do the history and the geography of the hungry grass.

PART I

Faith in Place

Land and Gospel

Seán Freyne

A region has been described by the Ulster poet John Hewitt as, 'a grouping smaller than the nation, larger than the family with which we could effectively identify, with which we could come to terms of sympathetic comprehension, within which our faculties and human potentialities could find due nurture and proper fulfilment. In short, the region is an area of a size and significance that we could hold in our hearts.'

Of course regionalism has quite different connotations when economists talk or politicians and their civil servants divide up the country for administrative reasons. It is in Hewitt's sense, not that of the bureaucrats, that we take Mayo to our hearts.

And yet we sometimes forget that our present county boundaries are man-made, in fact English in origin, intended deliberately to wipe out the older sense of the region defined in terms of the Gaelic provinces with their ancient traditions, legends and myths. Time has its own power of moulding the entities we create for purely pragmatic reasons into something greater, and history is full of ironies. Thus, today, there is no more powerful symbol of regional diversity in Ireland than the county boundaries, everything from Kerryman jokes to Donegal tweed. The Gaelic Athletic Association soon adopted the county as its primary unit, despite its continued espousal of the club-in-every-parish ideal. Gaelic revivalism thus made the English divisions of our country the corner-stone of its own organisation and thereby helped to bring about the sense of local identity that finds such passionate expression on our playing fields. The county has, despite occasional lingering nostalgia, replaced the province as 'the area that we can hold in our hearts'.

County boundaries are tangible realities on the football field or on motor-car registration plates. They are somewhat more difficult to define when one attempts to reflect on their theological significance. True, 'Mayo God help us' is now an honoured slogan that usually produces the retort that with the Reek and Knock we in Mayo have indeed been well looked after by the heavenly powers that be. But that simply begs the question whether there is any identifiable expression of faith and culture – for the two are inextricably intertwined – that could be labelled 'Mayo'? And if such an expression of our common inheritance can be discerned, what are the most likely factors, given our history and our landscape, that would have helped to bring that about? If that question appears at once too difficult and too obvious, we could perhaps turn it around and ask, what is there in our common inheritance as Christians that could and should have influenced our particular understanding of ourselves living and working in Mayo? Indeed once the problem has been articulated in this way, it becomes immediately obvious that both are simply different but complementary sides of the one question. The story must always remain primary for believers despite our attachments to Mayo and its story, yet the Mayo story will inevitably colour the way we see and hear the Christian story and single out certain aspects of it as particularly relevant. What follows is a brief reflection on one aspect of Mayo's story that is not prompted by one of Jesus' major concerns, namely, the significance of the land in human and religious terms.

Regionalism and the Gospel
Perhaps the most neglected, but for that reason none the less important, aspect of the gospel story is its regional character. Even the most passing acquaintance with any of our four gospels can immediately uncover the tensions within the story in terms of Galilee and Jeruslaem. Jesus is a Galilean, if not born, then certainly bred, a refugee to the north at an early age, it would appear.

While the gospel writers do not go in for too many details, the contrast clearly emerges and plays a significant role in the outcome: 'The Galileans accepted him.' (Jn 4:44) It is in Jerusalem that he was finally rejected. Accents are recognisably different and the landscape varies considerably from south to north, as reflected in the imagery. In Judea we encounter a barren fig-tree, whereas in Galilee there is a variety of soil, abundant harvests, plenty of fish to be caught in the lake and variegated flora and fauna, of which the famed 'lilies of the fields' are only one example among many. The population is engaged in different activities also. Fishermen, farmers and builders, in the main, people the Galilean section of the narrative, whereas in Jerusalem, the temple city, we meet those whose livelihood is dependent on the temple – priests, levites, scribes and a wide variety of service people, if we were to fill out the pictures from Jewish sources, – wood-cutters, incense-makers, innkeepers, those involved in animal slaughter, bakers ... In Galilee also one gets the distinct impression that the hard lines between Jew and non-Jew are considerably blurred. Jesus can attract crowds from all the surrounding regions and travels freely in non-Jewish territory whereas Jerusalem is the centre of orthodoxy, where those who set the standards as to what is and is not acceptable are centred. Not merely is Jerusalem the centre of religious control, it is also the place of real political power. In Jesus' day the Roman governor lived on the coast at Caesarea, but there was always a strong garrison to guard against any display of ultra-nationalism by overzealous Jews. Herod Antipas, the ruler of Galilee had, by contrast, a more benign image, despite his treatment of John the Baptist. Difficulties with his neighbours in Transjordan kept him fully occupied in that region. His building projects in Galilee, notably the cities of Sepphoris and Tiberias, were a major boost to the Galilean economy, but significantly, they were not centres of Jesus' preaching or healing activity.

The Galilee of Jesus was then essentially rural, though that does not mean that it was a backwater, either culturally or economically. As mentioned, the Herodian cities were a boost to the economy, irrespective of their somewhat alien character for country Jewish peasants. The villages were well stocked, and the natural resources of lake and fertile land fully exploited. Towns like Caphernaum, Bethsaida and Corozain, all mentioned in the gospels as places that, sadly, did not accept Jesus' message, were technically villages rather than cities, but we should think of them as having a population of ten to fifteen thousand rather than as mere hamlets. Their inhabitants would live off the land, owning their own plots or employed in the large estates that were also a feature of the economic pattern, either as service people or as tenant farmers. One ancient source speaks of as many as 60,000 vines having been planted in such an estate in lower Galilee, as well as an elaborate watering system. The Galileans, on the whole, were not poor – 'comfortable' as we would say in Mayo, even when the struggle for maintaining that position was never easy. Jesus' disciples could advise him to send away the crowds that followed him to the neighbouring towns and villages in order to buy food. Such a picture suggests that people had money, which in the ancient world meant that they were well up the social ladder, and that there was also a plentiful supply of goods available. There were times and places in Mayo of the last century where such an injunction would have been impracticable.

It was to these people, not to down and outs, and in these circumstances of relative affluence, that Jesus preached his message concerning the kingdom of God which proved in the end to be too radical, despite the initial enthusiasm with his healing ministry in particular. Even today, with all the advances in modern medical technology, the popular healer plays a social role that transcends class and culture. Much more so in the world of Jesus, where even Herod was anxious to see a healing miracle, not to speak of the woman who had spent all her possessions on doctors and was not the better for it!

At one level Jesus' understanding of God's kingly rule must have been attractive for the Galileans. The idea that God could be encountered away from Jerusalem would have meant a resolution of a genuine tension within their own social environment. The notion that the Divine Presence was somehow separate, localised in Jerusalem, created difficulties in day-to-day affairs of village and market when you lived in close physical proximity to Gentiles. The temple building, with its courtyards for various groups and its outer and inner sanctuaries, reflected a particular view not just of God's revelation to Israel but of Israel's relation to surrounding people. Through the Mediterranean world Jews had learned to accommodate their life style to a gentile environment and yet retain their own identity for centuries, but Galilee was different. It was close enough to be part of the land of Israel, yet, as a region it was much more in contact with the larger Greek world, linguistically and commercially, than Judea in the South or Jerusalem. Jesus' message that now all could share the same table irrespective of their ethnic or other background, because all were children of the same loving God, had, therefore, especially interesting possibilities for Galileans at a social as well as a religious level.

What then went wrong? Jesus never encountered serious hostility in Galilee; it was in Jerusalem that rejection came. Even his fellow Galilean pilgrims seem to have joined the mob calling for the end of this traitor, whereas his intimate band of Galilean followers tried to disguise both their origin and their links with him. However, one suspects that the parting of the ways, at least as far as Jesus was concerned, had come earlier. His ringing condemnation of the Galilean towns of Caphernaum, Bethsaida and Chorozain has all the echoes of the prophet not accepted in his own country. As pilgrims to Jerusalem the Galileans were giving expression to a deeply held conviction that the land which they inhabited had been given to them in stewardship by their God. Three times a year the faithful Israelite was expected to make the ascent, bringing with him offerings on behalf of himself and his family from his flocks and from the produce of his soil. In that climate people saw the land not just as theirs, received as an inheritance from their forebears, but as given to them as a gift from God - a sign of divine blessing and favour, whereas absence of this basic possession signalled rejection and disfavour. Jesus' lifestyle, precluding as it did any possessions, undertaken not out of necessity but out of conviction that such was the radical nature of God's call, was indeed a startling re-interpretation of his own people's understanding of where and how God's favour could be identified. In fact it stood that belief system on its very head. Nor was Jesus some kind of recluse who shunned society and opted for the desert; he conducted this mission in the very heartland of Galilee, warning these relatively comfortable people of the dangers of possessions in the name of the very God that they believed in, the God of Abraham, Isaac and Jacob. This God favoured outcasts, he declared, even sinners who previously were thought to have excluded themselves from the realm of God's care and love.

The message fell on deaf ears, not because the Galileans were bad people or unwilling to hear new ideas. It simply was too revolutionary, negating all their previous values and convictions. Perhaps those who had no stake in the land could hear and be encouraged; for those to whom the land was a way of life and the ultimate sign of God's favour, it made no sense. For professionals, like the scribes and the priests whose livelihood depended on the stability of those convictions, it was demonically inspired. For the few who accepted it on trust, however fearfully, it opened up horizons that changed their world completely, made them exiles in their own land, and transformed the name Galilean from a regional designation to a powerful symbol of the radically new way of human togetherness that had been disclosed to them in the life and death of Jesus, the Galilean.

Mayo's Struggle for the Land
In the light of this particular reading of the gospel story, one aspect of Mayo's history immediately springs to mind as offering an interesting point of intersection – the struggle for the land. The name of Mayoman Michael Davitt is synonymous with that struggle for ownership of the land, not just in Mayo but all over Ireland. Not that Davitt was alone, or indeed the first Mayoman to become involved in this issue. People like James Daly of Castlebar (the editor of the *Connaught Telegraph*), P.W.Nally (Balla) and J.O'Kane and J.P.Quinn (Claremorris) and J.J.Louden (Westport), were the immediate instigators of the movement to which Davitt lent his organisational skills and personal inspiration.

I often think that the frequent hassle over land in Ireland is due in no small part to the fact that we are such recent owners of land in our own country. It is as though the fear that we might lose what we have so recently acquired is deeply engrained in our collective psyche and hence the fierce struggle to protect our rights to the land. This is often symbolised, I think, in the amount of sweat and labour that has gone into fencing in even the smallest and most uninviting looking patches that dot the landscape in parts of Mayo at least. The more barren the soil the more vigorously we cling to it, as John B. Keane has so perceptively explored in *The Field*. For rural people land is an extension of themselves and they know themselves primarily in relation to it. This may sound an odd idea to the modern, sophisticated, urban mind, even primitive, yet on reflection it discloses a deep truth about ourselves as humans whether we are country or city people. All too frequently we know and define ourselves and others through what we and they own. Hence the drive in us to possess – the whole earth if it were decent and respectable to admit it. We have an insatiable desire to be owners of whatever is practical in our environment. Because of its primordial association with nature, the desire and need to own land is a powerful symbol of our human condition, beings of space as much as of time.

When the first meeting of what was later to become the Mayo Land League took place in Irishtown in 1879, it was necessity rather than abstract ideas that motivated those who called it, however. The movement was born of the injustices that had been perpetrated on Irish peasants and that threatened another great famine in that year. Davitt's own early experiences – eviction, exile, exploitation – had clearly sharpened his sense of social justice that demanded not just the three Fs (fair rent, fixity of tenure and freedom to dispose of their lease) but actual ownership of the land. The struggle in which Davitt became involved in his native Mayo on behalf of the tenant-farmers of Ireland has been described by his biographer-historian, the late T.W.Moody, as the greatest mass movement of protest in modern Ireland. It succeeded in uniting all shades of political and social opinion in the country on the basis of a sense of social justice that transcended all other issues and achieved its aims for the most part by peaceful means. Moody describes its tactics as follows: 'An elaborate system of moral-force warfare was developed; process-serving and evictions were made the occasion of great popular demonstrations; families evicted for non-payment of rents were sheltered and supported; an embargo was placed on evicted farms; persons involved in prosecutions because of their league activities were defended and the families of those sent to prison cared for, and the terrible weapon of social ostracisation, the boycott, was perfected as the ultimate sanction of the league against all persons who violated its code.' (*The Course of Irish History*, 280)

Ownership of their own land was not a matter of abstract principle but of genuine necessity for survival for the Irish peasants of the 19th century. The great famine of the 1840s, and its near repeat in 1879, are all too poignant witness to that fact. It is interesting that it was to his native county that Davitt returned to lend his considerable gifts of personality and leadership to the cause of Irish tenant farmers after his broadening and radicalising experiences in a British gaol and in America. The prophet must be rooted in the people and yet the vision is always greater than their immediate needs. Davitt was certainly a prophet of social justice in 1879 and in the years immediately thereafter.

Mayo people are rightly proud of the achievement of Michael Davitt, and of their forebears under his direction in our county over a hundred years ago, with the peaceful mass meetings at Irishtown, Claremorris, Shrule, Westport, Ballyhaunis, Tuam, Headford, Ballinrobe, Annaghdown and Newport. And yet one wonders if this historic movement, so ably recalled in various centenary celebrations in Straide and elsewhere throughout the county just a few years ago, might not be in danger of turning into nostalgia in our collective memories, as our county and country move rapidly away from the patterns of subsistence farming that operated here until so recently. Perhaps a critical reflection on its enduring significance in the light of the other story about land which we have been considering, and which our Christian faith tells us has enduring meaning, might save it from a fate worse than death – remembrance without commitment to its ideals and goals. Davitt and the Mayo Land League deserve to remain with us as inspirations for the future we hope to create together, rather than as dead memories from the past.

Immediately we see the contrasts between the two stories. Jesus warned people that land and possessions had no absolute character as signs of God's favour, indeed were in danger of distorting a true understanding of the human condition, whereas Davitt's movement was a statement that without ownership of land there was no possibility of meaningful existence for the people at large. This basic contrast does not, however, amount to opposition between the two visions. The Mayo peasants had a sub-human existence and the movement to which Davitt lent his support based its claim on the belief 'that the land belonged to the people' and was 'intended by a just and all-providing God for the sustenance of the people to whom he gave inclination and energy to cultivate and improve it'. It was not to be used as a usurious monopoly by an elite landlord caste. Social justice, therefore, basic human rights, demanded that the land and its fruits should belong to the people. In the political climate of the day that meant private ownership, not just a fair rent or fixed tenure, since experience had taught how fragile those conditions could be, depending on the whims of individual landlords. Jesus' call was made, not in the context of landlord exploitation, though there was some of that in Galilee also, but on the understanding that God's care extends to all, irrespective of their possessions, and that all alike share the common dignity and status of children of God, irrespective of what they own. Indeed, non-ownership only highlights the blessedness of those whose trust is in God, not in food, drink or clothing, according to Jesus' famous Sermon on the Mount. These have achieved the inner freedom that makes love of others possible because the deep-seated anxieties that every human being is faced with, and which possessions help to assuage, have been overcome by trust in a greater power than 'self', namely a loving and caring God.

Unlike many of the mass movements of liberation occurring today against a background of human greed and exploitation, as in

Latin America, the Philippines and South Africa, the Mayo land leaguers did not take their inspiration from the gospels but from the principles of natural justice as enunciated by the British liberal philosopher/economist, John Stuart Mill. Perhaps it was good strategy to address their claims to the British Parliament in such an idiom. The fact is, however, that neither Catholic social theory, nor indeed Catholic theology generally, was at that time capable of expressing a vision of Gospel justice that could have been a powerful stimulus to Davitt and his followers. Though many of the clergy supported the movement, while attempting to exercise a restraining hand, there is at least the suggestion that the Irishtown meeting was called as a protest against the local parish priest who was administering the family estates and reluctant to reduce the rent despite the desperate plight of the tenants that particular year, due to the inclement weather and the failure of the crops. In what is suspected not to have been his own view but that of his secretary, the ageing John McHale, Archbishop of Tuam condemned the movement as the work of a few unprincipled people who sought to drive a wedge between clergy and people. Unlike the Second Vatican Council of our own times, the first Vatican Council of 1870 was inward looking, concerned with ecclesiastical authority rather than with world issues of peace and justice. It would be another ten years before a new Pope, Leo XIII, would begin to articulate a Catholic theory of social justice that has reached its flowering in our day with the remarkable, though often ignored, social teaching of recent Popes, particularly of Pope John XXIII.

In truth what the Land Leaguers were asking for was no more than basic justice, without which it is impossible for people to begin to hear the call of Jesus to that greater freedom which does not see the ultimate goal of human life in acquiring possessions. The way of Jesus only becomes a practicable possibility in all its radicalness when there is a communal sense of human togetherness and sharing. In such an atmosphere of trust in one another, it is possible to transcend the drives for self-preservation and aggrandisement that seem to be so endemic to the human condition at the personal, familial and even national level. Mutual trust and support leads to a deeper sense of trust and the realisation that people, not possessions, are what human life is about. This in turn leads to the conviction that a personal, caring God, a father and a mother figure, holds our lives and our universe together, despite the often contradictory signs that we encounter.

Did Mayo, then, and indeed Ireland, lose its opportunity to develop its own liberation theology by having its social revolution too soon? Many of its daughters and sons are today in the forefront of the struggle for justice in far-flung missionary fields in Africa,

Asia and Latin America, their inspiration coming not from the struggles of their native Mayo a century ago, but from the story of a Galilean visionary nineteen centuries earlier. The Land League's aspirations and tactics did achieve a certain degree of gospel-togetherness among the Mayo peasants, even when this was not explicitly the source of its inspiration. Like every social revolution, the Land War represented an end and a beginning. The struggle of the tenant farmers of the 19th century was followed in the 20th by the struggle of the urban workers in the labour movement of Larkin and Connolly. It is one of the sad ironies of modern Ireland that historically there were few links between the two struggles, the one rural, the other urban. The lack of impact of the one on the other is shown in the absence of any great solidarity between these two constituencies today, at a time when a new wave of economic hardship of a very different kind is affecting both country and city alike, with devastating effects, denuding the countryside of its young life and creating an alienated and marginalised working class in our cities and larger towns. Thus, the struggle for social justice must continue in town and country, and we today have a much broader repertoire of resources than did our forebears one hundred odd years ago with which to engage in that struggle. Not least of these is the recovery of the social dimensions of the gospel of Jesus the Galilean, that was first expressed and lived in conditions not dissimilar to those of Mayo, and indeed rural Ireland generally, almost two thousand years ago.

The Jesus revolution on the whole was a failure in his native Galilee. Behind the slogan 'the prophet is not accepted in his own country' lies a whole range of complex social realities that made the message too radical, as we have tried to indicate. Country people can be self-sufficient in ways that are not just about bread and butter. Having one's own place can make one smug, parochial, even downright uncaring. 'I'm all right, Jack' is not just an urban philosophy, despite the sharing that can go on between neighbours of the same social level in the countryside. The *meitheal* philosophy, romantic though it appears at a distance, had its strict boundaries of reciprocity: do for others what you want them to do for you. For the Galilean peasants the three annual pilgrimages to Jerusalem were intended as reminders that there was a greater world than theirs and that the land had been given to them in trust for all Israel. The tithes and other agricultural offerings were supposed to be a very tangible reminder of that fact. The pilgrimage should never have allowed them to turn their own regional identity into a sense of exclusiveness that ignored the fact of belonging to the larger Jewish and human families. Yet, in rejecting the vision of Jesus, they opted for a self-destructive isolation that found its expression in two disastrous wars against Rome, inspired by narrow nationalism. It was throughout the cities of the Greco-Roman world that those Galileans who followed Jesus were to sow the fruitful seeds of the alternative vision that was first expressed in rural Galilee.

There is perhaps another way for us Mayo people to be challenged by our places of pilgrimage, namely, by approaching them from the perspective of our past struggle for the land and all that that implied then and demands of us now. The Mayo Land League was a shining example of a mass movement for social justice dismantling what must have appeared an immovable system of oppression – by peaceful means. The Mayo Land League was soon transformed into a national movement, reaching out beyond the boundaries of the county – a region's gift to the whole people. Today, at the Reek and Knock we meet people from every corner of Ireland and beyond, people from city and country alike and of every social class, all engaged in a common search for something greater and more significant for their lives. Our call as Christians today must surely be to reach out beyond ourselves and join with all pilgrims in a common struggle for a justice that is all-inclusive, based on Jesus' call and the Jesus way. Building on our successful struggles for justice in Mayo, but not bound by past successes, we must help to fashion a new Ireland, by being particularly sensitive to the needs of those who never had and never will have their own 'half-acre', and who are most vulnerable to the particular economic pressures of our day. It would be a very unfortunate consequence indeed were those, who have places of pilgrimage within their very region, to miss out on being pilgrims themselves, to be Jerusalemites rather than Galileans, or if the children of those who struggled successfully for justice a century ago were to become insensitive to the demands of justice in their own day, precisely because of their attachment to the fruits of those successes. According to Jesus' story we are all pilgrims together, and that is why our Mayo story – indeed all our stories personal, regional and national – must always remain unfinished stories for those who take seriously in their lives the story and the struggle of the Galilean pilgrim of long ago.

Faith and Fear: The Christian Disciple

Michael Neary

Faith is associated with journey, progress and pilgrimage. Fear expresses itself in stagnation and regression. Faith enables us to move ourselves. As Christians, we are a mixture of faith and fear, of progress and stagnation.

As we reflect on what the gospels have to say about the disciples, we get an insight, not just into that group which followed Jesus, but also an understanding and awareness of ourselves as Christian men and women. Reading what the gospels have to say about the group which followed Jesus is like looking into a mirror. The difficulties which the early disciples had are our difficulties and we can identify with them, whether in faith or fear.

Geography
Our geographical situation contributes to making us the type of people we are and frequently determines our reactions. Mayo people, growing up as we do, close to the mountains and the sea, find the planes of Meath and Kildare monotonous and even oppressive. Failure to take cognizance of the geographical setting of the Holy Land has made our reading of the gospels more difficult, and in many cases, has in fact militated against our understanding of the ministry and message of Jesus. Palestine was a tiny country in the east of the Roman empire. It was strategically situated at the meeting point of the three continents, Europe, Asia and Africa.

The country was surrounded by hostile forces, by the Syrians to the north, the Assyrians to the north-east, Babylonians to the east and Egyptians to the south. There was a great temptation to compromise with the prevailing power of the day. The prophets, for seven hundred years before Christ, had counselled reliance on God rather then alliance with powerful neighbours. Israel experienced the bitterness of landlessness, of being totally exposed, helpless and victimised. Five hundred years before the time of Christ the people were deported to Babylon. They were a broken, beaten, betrayed people. Yet in that situation of helplessness, they discovered new depths of support in their faith and new dimensions to their idea of God. In our own country, the Penal Laws (1691-1760) were calculated to destroy the Catholic faith but in fact they had quite the opposite effect. Since then our people experienced the depths to which landlordism stooped in Mayo, but what is more interesting is the way which landlessness caused the people to summon up their reserves and respond, in terms of the non-violent yet powerful protest of Michael Davitt and the Land League, and in terms of a more specifically religious response on the part of Knock, Archbishop John McHale and, in our own day, Fr John Blowick and Monsignor James Horan.

The land of Palestine from north to south measured about one hundred and sixty miles (roughly Castlebar to Cork). From east to west it varies from thirty miles in the north, to about fifty miles in the south (roughly Achill to Charlestown). There are striking similarities between Ireland and Israel in history, culture and religion. About nine hundred years before Christ, the land had been divided into two Kingdoms, north and south. The results of that division were evident in Jesus' time.

Moving from west to east it is customary to divide Palestine into four areas. Firstly, a narrow coastal plain along the Mediterranean, secondly a central mountain range running north-south which incorporates the mountains of Judea, thirdly the valley of the river Jordan, and finally the mountains east of Jordan which run north-south. The Sea of Galilee is a heart-shaped lake measuring about eight by thirteen miles. It was in the vicinity of that lake that Jesus conducted his public ministry, moving only to Jerusalem for the final few days before his passion. This then is the country the boundaries of which Jesus scarcely traversed during his lifetime.

The ministry of Jesus is presented in terms of a journey from Galilee in the north, to Jerusalem in the south. This is more than a geographical journey. Geography is used as a vehicle by the gospel writers to convey a theological message, that is, a message about God, humankind and the drama of salvation.

Galilee was more open to foreign influences. The great trade route linking the Babylonian and Egyptian empires passed through that area. The fertile plains of Galilee made it the bread basket of Israel. In Old Testament times wars were fought in that part. As a result the area was recognised as containing a mixed population. It was seen as a place which was therefore lukewarm in matters of faith and a hot-bed for any revolutionary movement. But significantly it was there that Jesus spent the first part of his public ministry.

Jerusalem, in the south, by contrast is self-sufficient, self-righteous and introverted. It is the place of the establishment. The centre of Jewish worship, the Temple is located there. Jerusalem and the priests associated with it do not wish to be challenged. The prophets were seen as the ones who challenged the men and women of the time to live according to the law of the Lord. Jesus has a good idea of what awaits him in that city as he challenges the people and their priests with fidelity to God's ways. There Jesus spends that last week of his earthly life.

FAITH AND FEAR: THE CHRISTIAN DISCIPLE

PART I: GALILEE: THE TEMPTATION OF THE TWELVE

That is the background against which Jesus and the twelve interact. The call of the twelve by Jesus, in Mk 3:13-19, is due to his initiative. 'He called whom he desired; and they came to him.' A relationship is set up. They are called for a twofold purpose 'to be with him and to be sent out to preach.' It is interesting to note the various types reflected in those called. Peter, the impetuous, could even be an Irishman! The country of Palestine was under Roman occupation at the time. Matthew the tax-collector would be seen as a representative of Roman Rule. Tax-collecting was auctioned off so it made dishonesty second nature. Matthew would be seen as an extortionist in the eyes of many. By contrast there is Simon the Zealot. The Zealots were a group of fanatical nationalists. If slogans were fashionable at the time, theirs would have been 'Romans out.' James and John are numbered among the twelve, the ones who were ambitious for the top posts. Thomas the doubter, Andrew the practical man, and Judas the cautious, all so different in character, temperament and outlook; yet they are all drawn to Jesus. What you have in that group is a mini-church with the characteristics and polarities which we find in ourselves and in the church today.

Simon's name is changed to Peter. Whenever you get a name change in the Bible it is indicative of a new relationship with the one who changes the name. Abram's name was changed to Abraham in the book of Genesis, Saul to Paul in the Acts of the Apostles. Peter will be called by this name right through the gospel of Mark with one significant exception. In Gethsemane when Jesus finds him sleeping, he addresses him, 'Simon, are you asleep?' (Mk 14:37) In other words Peter, in his failure to be alert, has fallen back into his pre-call state and so he has failed in discipleship. As disciples we too are called to be vigilant. Have we allowed exploitation and manipulation to take place in politics, the business world or family structures? Have we been indifferent when injustice was perpetrated around us?

The disciples in Mark chapter three were chosen for a twofold purpose, 'to be with Jesus, and to be sent out to preach.' Being with Jesus is their primary mission. In their being with him they become involved in his mission and their apostolate is founded on their relationship with him. The interaction between Jesus and the twelve in this gospel is very interesting and provides today's disciple with hope. The disciples are constantly with Jesus and their relationship with him matures in different ways.

In the first part of his ministry, the disciples readily identify with a Jesus who promises much but seems to demand little. The bandwagon is rolling and they are anxious to be on it and to bask in the acclaim of the miracle worker. There is a certain security in the tried and tested. We can verify this from our own experience. But once we move away from the familiar there is risk involved, the risk of being hurt, rejected, misinterpreted. We can see this tension illustrated in the story of the calming of the storm in Mt 8: 18-27. Jesus is teaching about discipleship and invites would-be disciples to follow him. Following Jesus becomes a technical term for discipleship. The story of the calming of the storm commences. 'And when Jesus got into the boat his disciples followed him.' (Mt 8:23) This story then is intended to be read as a story about discipleship. It captures our experience today. The church, a boat on the storm-tossed seas of the world, an apparently sleeping Jesus, fearful disciples who panic. Like the disciples in the story we today are a combination of faith and fear. 'Why are you afraid, you of little faith?' were the words addressed to them by Jesus. In the church today many feel we are coping with a sleeping Jesus who does not show his presence or power. In our own lives we may be confronted by an eclipse of God. Yet Christ is present and in control even as the storm rages. The disciples turn to Jesus in that crisis. A crisis may send us in either of two directions, causing us to turn to God in faith for help, and so leading to a deepening of our vacillating faith, or it may cause us to throw our religious beliefs overboard and abandon faith.

In the first part of the ministry of Jesus, his disciples misinterpret and misunderstand. Peter, their leader, is reluctant to allow Jesus to retreat for a period of quiet prayer and reprimands him, 'everyone is searching for you.' (Mk 1:37) Peter, like the rest, wants a miracle-worker who will remain at centre-stage and ensure that the spotlight is always on the group. The twelve have preconceived ideas of Jesus as a political liberator and fail to push beyond that. We can detect a certain impatience and frustration building up in Jesus as he fires rapid questions at them. 'Why do you discuss the fact that you have no bread? Do you not perceive or understand? Are your hearts hardened? Having eyes do you not see and having ears do you not hear? And do you not remember? When I broke the five loaves for the five thousand, how many baskets full of broken pieces did you take up?' And they said to him, 'seven'. And he said to them, 'do you not yet understand?' (Mk 8:17-21)

PART II: JOURNEY TO JERUSALEM

The second part of the ministry of Jesus involves a journey to Jerusalem. This demands leaving behind the success and the miracle-working of Galilee and moving in the direction of Jerusalem and the cross. The journey is not merely geographical, it is highly theological, a journey back to the Father. It is our journey through life. Jesus is aware that the disciples want a glorious liberator but he proceeds to educate them in the meaning of suffering and the cross. He recognises that the disciples are guilty of a lack of faith which is a form of blindness that must be healed. The first section of his ministry highlighted this misunderstanding, lack of faith and blindness on the part of the disciples.

It is hardly surprising that the theme of blindness is taken up again in the second part of his ministry. Two stories of restoration of sight to blind people (Mk 8:22-26 and Mk 10:46-52) serve to bracket a central section of the gospel and provide us with a key to interpreting the material contained between those stories. In Mk 8:22-26 Jesus takes the blind man by the hand, leads him out of the village and the miracle then takes place in two stages. Jesus places spittle on the eyes of the blind man and lays his hands upon him asking him if he saw anything. 'I see men, but they look like trees, walking,' was the reply. Then Jesus laid his hands upon his eyes and the blind man looked intently and was restored, and saw everything clearly. This is the only miracle in the New Testament when Jesus is not successful at the first attempt. Mark uses the story to illustrate the difficulty which Jesus has in removing the blindness, the lack of faith on the part of the disciples. Notice that in curing the blind man Jesus takes him away from the familiar, from the tried and tested. This calls for faith in the one who leads. Jesus is doing something similar with his disciples as he leads them away from the glorious miracle-working of Galilee to Jerusalem. As disciples today we have to reflect on the way he leads us into unknown and unfamiliar areas in our lives.

The second miracle of restoration of sight is recounted in Mk 10:46-52. Significantly this story immediately follows on the request of James and John for positions of influence alongside Jesus. Jesus asks the blind man the identical question which he had asked of James and John, 'What do you want me to do for you?' (10:36-51) But whereas the blind man answers, 'Master let me receive my sight,' James and John answer, 'grant us to sit, one at your right, and one at your left in your glory.' Mark stresses that immediately the blind man received his sight he followed Jesus 'on the way' (10:52), that is, on the way to Jerusalem and the cross. In other words the blind man becomes a true disciple.

Between these two stories of the restoration of sight we see Jesus trying to remove the blindness of the disciples. Different manifestations of their blindness surface. The first misunderstanding or distortion of meaning is seen in the confession of Peter at Caesarea Philippi, 'you are the Christ.' (Mk 8:29) The right words are used, but this confession is something of a half truth. He is the great messianic liberator, but Jesus considers it necessary to fill out the meaning of this confession by introducing the idea of his suffering, 'and he began to teach them that the Son of Man must suffer many things, and be rejected by the elders and the chief priests and the scribes and be killed and after three days rise again.' (Mk 8:13) As soon as Peter hears that suffering is part of Jesus' vocation he immediately tries to divert him from that path. This provokes a stern reaction, 'Get behind me Satan for you are not on the side of God but men.' (8:33) It is worth noting that Peter is the only character in the gospels who is identified as a satanic personality, and he is identified as such by Jesus. Peter is anxious to call the shots, to dictate terms for the Messiah and decide how discipleship should be lived. The selection process is at work. Peter must learn to 'get behind' Jesus and follow16 him; he must learn to be a disciple.

Another manifestation of the disciples' misunderstanding may be seen in the raw ambition which surfaces. Jesus is involved in a very intense education programme with the twelve. Mark says, 'they went on from there and passed through Galilee. And he would not have anyone know it; for he was teaching his disciples.' (Mk 9:30-31) For the second time he spells out specifically his future suffering. Immediately after this second passion prediction, we find the disciples discussing among themselves who was the greatest (Mark 9:34). They are on a totally different wave-length. Personal power and prestige is their primary preoccupation. This results in a domineering and exclusive mentality on their part. They try to ensure that exorcism will be an exclusive preserve of their own and so they endeavour to prevent any exorcist, who is not one of their number, from functioning. They try to dominate Jesus by deciding who would have access to him. Although Jesus had emphasised the importance of receiving the Kingdom as a little child, the disciples prevent people bringing little children to him for a blessing. Mark sums up the reaction of the disciples in terms of misunderstanding and fearful inhibition to ask for a solution.

During the passion, fear on the part of the disciples reaches a crescendo. In Gethsemane Mark emphasises the isolation of Jesus. The disciple is one who leaves all to follow Jesus, but when the crisis comes a young man leaves everything to escape and runs away naked. (Mk 14:51-52) Mark's final word on their behaviour during the arrest is 'they all forsook him and fled,' (14:50) in other words the twelve deny the first purpose for which they were called, namely to be 'with Jesus'. Peter follows Jesus at a distance into the courtyard of the high priest. The camera focuses first'y on the trial of Jesus upstairs. The high priest questions him, 'are you the Christ the Son of the Blessed?' to which Jesus replies, 'I am.' (14:61-62) At the same time in the courtyard below, one of the maid-servants of the high priest accuses Peter of being a disciple of Jesus, 'you also were with the Nazarene, Jesus,' but Peter vehemently denies and disowns him. (Mk 14:66-72) So at the very moment when Jesus identifies with men, Peter is denying his discipleship.

Feminine Faith

The most frequently repeated command in the bible is 'fear not', 'be not afraid.' Faith courageously sets out towards the promised land; fear causes us to hold on to anything we can get hold of. While faith provides the courage to let go, fear causes us to cling. In that respect fear, rather than doubt, is the opposite of faith. Mark's gospel was written probably in Rome about 70 A.D., a time of intense persecution for the followers of Christ as the grim terror of Nero stalked the streets of that city. Understandably the evangelist is very concerned about fear. In very subtle ways he illustrates how faith conquers fear, particularly in the case of some women.

Disciples are called upon to follow Jesus. In contrast to the rich young man, who kept all the commandments and who could not accept the cost and part with his possessions (10:17-22), we have the story of the poor widow who gives everything to God (12:41-44). As he is about to recount the story of the Passion of Jesus, Mark inserts the story of another woman who anoints Jesus at Bethany (Mk 14:3). We have seen the difficulty which the twelve in general, and Peter in particular, had in making the connection between confessing Jesus as Messiah and his suffering and death. The woman at Bethany who anoints Jesus makes the connection; she anoints him with a view to his death. She is presented as the ideal, namely, as one who understands who Jesus is and responds with total self-giving.

There is a sense in which Mark causes the gospel to depend on the women who were witnesses, namely on Mary Magdalene and the other women. The twelve, as we have seen, had abandoned Jesus at the arrest (14:50). Mark is careful to note that the women were witnesses not only of Jesus' death (15:40) but also of his burial place (15:47) and later of the empty tomb (16:1-6). These women have qualified to become disciples. They 'followed' Jesus and 'came up with him to Jerusalem' (Mk 15:40-44). 'There were also women looking on from afar, among whom were Mary Magdalene, and Mary the mother of James the younger and of Joseph, and Salome, who, when he was in Galilee, followed him and ministered to him, and also many other women who came up with him to Jerusalem' (Mk 15:40-41).

The women are given a mandate after the resurrection: they are to tell the disciples that Jesus goes before them and will meet them in Galilee (16:7). However they did not carry out that mandate; 'they went out and fled from the tomb; for trembling and astonishment had come upon them; and they said nothing to anyone, for they were afraid.' (16:8) This is the real ending of Mark's gospel. By concluding in such a way, the evangelist may well be illustrating that God's plan will be victorious despite the contradiction of the cross and the failure and lack of faith on the part of the disciples, whether the misunderstanding of the men or the weakness of the women.

Conclusion

The disciples then are presented by Mark as lacking in faith, filled with anxious self-concern, obtuse and incorrigible. Yet Jesus persists and perseveres with them. In this gospel, whenever Jesus is rejected he counteracts by taking a new initiative. In the Synagogue at Capernaum his rejection results in his calling of the disciples, while the rejection at Nazareth leads to the sending of the disciples out on mission. When the final rejection comes during the passion, Jesus responds by promising he will meet them in Galilee after his resurrection (Mk 14:27-28). This means that the final word on discipleship is not failure or frustration but forgiveness and reconciliation. In his portrayal of the disciples, Mark wishes the reader of his gospel to identify with the disciples in their fear, frailty and weakness, in their mistakes and misunderstandings. But no matter what our failure, irrrespective of our past, there is always the possibility of repentance and a new future, of faith overcoming fear. Jesus chooses the most unlikely material when he selects his disciples, so if we happen to fall into that category there is hope.

What application has this for Mayo men and women today? Because our culture has had a long investment in family life, one expects a strong reaction to the contemporary crisis. Educational opportunities are probably more available in Mayo than ever before, yet unemployment and emigration have created tension, fear and hardship for family life and for faith. We become either the victims or beneficiaries of the change in society. When change becomes threatening we tend to retract and resist. Knock airport has provided a window on the world. Today Mayo is less than an hour from Manchester and a little more from London. The sociological supports, on which faith frequently depended in rural Ireland, are now being quickly eroded. We can either lament the change, indulge in a whining self-pity, or we can grasp the opportunity to deepen our faith in a God who leads us, as he has lead his disciples in the past, away from the familiar of the tried and tested to explore new heights and experience new dimensions of his support, where the scales of blindness will be removed.

Sacrament of God

Enda Lyons

I

The surveys on sacramental practice in Ireland always surprise me. The situation, it would appear, is not after all as bad as I would have thought. The level of practice, the statistics assure us, is remarkably high 'even among young people.' However, no matter what the surveys tell us, we all know deep down that something strange is happening in sacramental practice today.

Nobody can deny, for example, the dramatic decline in confessions in recent years. Even where churches are still filled for Sunday Mass, few can have excaped noticing that the remark, 'I find Mass boring,' is being heard more and more frequently.

Nor, indeed, is everything well with baptism. In regard to this sacrament, the fears that go with an old theology die slowly and, whether we like it or not, very many people are still left deeply influenced by the threat to their child of an eternity in Limbo if original sin is not removed by baptism, a threat which, indeed, even official documents seem slow to remove. So, generally speaking, parents still have the child baptised ('done', as is often said.). But often the child is baptised, I think, with less conviction and with perhaps more superstition – 'just in case anything might happen to the child and we would have to live with our fears and our regrets for the rest of our days.'

The crisis in sacramental practice, of which there are these and other signs, is, of course, linked with and part of the wider crisis of religious belief today – a crisis arising to a large extent from the need, and often the failure, to find belief again in 'a brave new world', and to understand it in a contemporary way. But within this wider crisis, the sacraments are undergoing a crisis of their own, one which has its roots in our understanding and experience of the sacraments themselves. In particular, it seems to me, it has its roots in the fact that sacraments are not seen to have a context in our everyday experience of life.

It is true to say, I believe, that when we Catholics hear the word 'sacrament', we think immediately of 'the seven sacraments' of our Church. These we understand as seven sacred rites 'instituted by Christ for our salvation.' Sacrament, then, is seen as something altogether novel, introduced into human life by Christ, almost out of the blue. It is not seen as arising out of our experience of life generally, nor, even after being introduced by Christ, is it seen as fitting in easily with the rest of our experience. Being then like nothing else in life, it is thought of as being, literally, like nothing on earth. And so, in a world in which, it is often said, we have 'come of age' and of which, through science and technology, we have, in one sense at least, become more in control, sacrament becomes an increasingly isolated concept and one in which it is increasingly difficult to believe. Sacrament more and more smacks of magic. Magic is something in which we do not believe, and in which we ought not to believe.

One of the great needs today in this regard is to ground sacraments in our everyday experience and to give them a home and a context in our everday life. Our interest then should be, not first of all in 'the sacraments', but in the much broader reality of *sacramentality*. This latter is a feature of our whole life and is not just confined to seven 'churchy' moments of it. This is the human context out of which 'the sacraments' arise, into which they fit and in which alone they make sense.

II

We begin to appreciate sacramentality when we begin to appreciate 'symbol'. We begin to appreciate symbol by reflecting on an aspect of our everyday experience. Part of our experience is that reality is not purely superficial but can have a depth dimension – that there is more to it than meets the eye. It is to express this feature of life that the word symbol is used. The following sentence from Roger Hazelton describes symbol well: 'There is more than appears on the surface, and yet the surface is where the depth begins to appear.'[1] Since symbol is a feature of our everyday experience, everyday examples abound. One simple example is the spoken word. There is more to this than the sound which appears on the surface: there is also the meaning which the sound can convey. Anyone who can hear at all, even a baby, can experience the sound itself. But only those who are able, not just to hear, but also to understand, can get beneath the surface and experience the meaning of the word. Take away the sound, however, and the meaning ceases to be conveyed – 'the surface is where the depth begins to appear.'

Another everyday example is the human body. There is more to this than appears on the surface: there is the person embodied here. And yet it is only in and through the body that the person 'begins to appear'.

A final homely example is a warm handshake. There is more happening here than two people just squeezing each other's hands: in and through this physical contact there is deep communication going on – something inward, sympathy or support or shared joy, is being signified and actually conveyed.

It is often thought that a symbol is 'only a sign' – so much so that both terms, sign and symbol, are frequently mentioned in the one breath as though they were synonymous. A symbol is indeed a sign, because it always points to the existence of something beyond. But it is not 'a *mere* sign' in that it does not just point to something *outside* itself, as a sign-post does to the next town. A symbol makes present the reality to which it points, as a body gives presence to the person it embodies; a symbol conveys the reality which it signifies, as a word conveys meaning; a symbol is the instrument through which that which is expressed is also communicated, as the handshake is the instrument through which support or sympathy is communicated.

How this has to do with *sacrament* ought to become clear when we consider some 'old' truths about sacraments. Sacrament, the catechism told us, is ' an outward sign of inward grace.' Sacrament, according to another telling, is 'a sign and instrument of grace.' Heavy theological language, this. But the reality to which it refers is not really as alien to our experience as the language might suggest.

The word 'grace', of course, immediately creates a problem and calls for comment, if only in passing. It suggests some mysterious spiritual liquid which can be poured into souls and found there in greater or lesser quantities. But the word 'grace' is, of course, connected with the word graciousness. It is the fruit of God's graciousness – it is gift or favour. Theology might indeed have used the word 'grace' to refer to everything we have, since, we believe, everything is God's gift. In fact, however, theology reserved the word for the most astonishing and amazing of all God's gifts, that is the gift of family-intimacy with God, the gift of being able to address and relate to God, not just as Creator, but ,with Jesus, as Abba. For 'grace' then, in the above definitions of sacrament, we might substitute 'intimate love'. In that case, according to the catechism, sacrament is a sign ('outward') of God's intimate love. According to the other telling referred to, it is a sign of God's intimate love for us and also an instrument through which this love is bestowed on us. It is some thing, or person, which is 'laden with divine power'.[2]

For a moment, we may ignore the word 'divine' in this phrase. Insofar as sacrament is some gesture or person or thing laden with power beyond itself, insofar as it is something to which 'there is more than appears on its surface and yet the surface is where the depth begins to appear,' it is not at all foreign to our experience. It belongs to the world of symbol – *our* world. It is this – our world of symbol, our everyday world where there is far more to things than meets the eye – and not the catechism or the church or 'the sacraments', which has to be our point of entry into the world of sacrament. Our point of entry has to be the wedding ring put on the finger of the spouse on the wedding day – an 'outward' sign of an inner reality. It has to be the squeeze of a hand when we visit the house of a bereaved neighbour – a sign of heartfelt sympathy and an instrument through which it is conveyed. It has to be the familiar experience of three pieces of cloth, green, white and orange, or two pieces, red and green, sewn together and embodying the hopes and the strivings and the successes and the failures of a nation or a county – objects laden with power, especially when flown at the right time in the right place or, equally, at the wrong time in the wrong place. Awareness of and sensitivity to the fact that the place where we live is one in which 'there is more than appears on its surface and yet the surface is where the depth begins to appear' will not automatically give us the insight required to appreciate the Christian notion of sacrament. But without this awareness and sensitivity we will never understand this notion at all. Awareness of the symbolic nature of the world around us is our first step towards understanding sacrament.

III

The second step is a more difficult one and one which we are often tempted to avoid. It is the step which brings us into the world of religion itself – a necessary step surely, for one who would appreciate the religious significance of such relatively esoteric religious rites as 'the sacraments'.

Religious belief (which, of course, did not begin with Christianity but which is as old as history) is basically *insight* – insight into the 'religious' dimension of our experience. How *much* more, we might ask, is there to life than appears on its surface? *How* deep is the depth which only begins to appear there? Is the 'more' which begins to appears on the surface just a little more or even just a lot more? The peculiar insight which is the basis of religious belief perceives in life hints of what is literally immeasurably more than appears on the surface, echoes of depths beginning to appear there which are literally unfathomable. Religious belief is aware of the puzzling nature of life – its tragedy and its comedy, its joys and its pains, its hopes and its fears, its successes and its failures, its love and its hate, its beauty and its ugliness, its capacity for good and evil, its ability to think both the most noble and the most ignoble thoughts. But it perceives that '... in all our thought and language there is a resonance of the Infinite, as its deepest background ...'[3] It perceives the horizons of our experience, with all its puzzle, indeed precisely because of all its puzzle, as being, in Tennyson's words:

> an arch wherethrough
> Gleams that untravelled world whose margin fades
> For ever and for ever when I move. [4]

Religious belief is basically a conviction that there are, in our experience of life, hints of that Fulness which we call 'God' – a Reality which reflects the puzzling nature of our experience or, rather, of which the puzzling nature of our experience is itself a reflection; a Reality which, paradoxically, is totally beyond our grasp yet is deeply involved with us and is involving us with Itself; a Reality which, in Karl Rahner's words, is both 'infinitely distant' and yet is '... what is most internal to ourselves,'[5]; a 'mystery', to use Rudolf Otto's language, which is both awesome and alluring (*tremendum et fascinans*).[6] Religious belief is basically a conviction that there are, in life, hints and intimations of that 'Presence' of which Wordsworth had an unusually intense experience above Tintern Abbey:

> ... And I have felt
> A presence that disturbs me with the joy
> Of elevated thoughts; a sense sublime
> Of something far more deeply interfused,
> Whose dwelling is the light of setting suns,
> And the round ocean and the living air,
> And the blue sky, and in the mind of man:
> A motion and a spirit, that impels
> All thinking things, all objects of all thought ... [7]

Religious belief is a perception of life being laden, not just with power, but with *divine* power; as being an 'outward sign' of *divine* presence; as being, in Gerald Manley Hopkins' phrase, 'charged with the grandeur of God.'[8] It is a conviction that, to recall Joseph Mary Plunkett, Blood can be seen upon the rose, and Eyes in the stars, and Tears falling from the skies.[9] Or, to recall Patrick Kavanagh, that Someone can indeed be seen coming in a January flower.[10] In other words, it is an understanding of life as being a symbol or sacrament of God.

This religious insight, though available to all, does not come automatically or always easily. Certainly it cannot be arrived at just be learning doctrine by rote – no more than can the insight into the deeper meaning and beauty of music or art or poetry be arrived at simply in this way.

Reflection is necessary – reflection on, for example, the superabundance of which the beauty of a person or a thing is suggestive; or on the boundless ocean onto which we launch when we begin to think of that with which the human spirit can be concerned.[11]

Listening is necessary – listening, for example, to those deep sounds which can really be heard only in silence.

And *doing* is necessary – responding, for example, to the cry of the poor ones in our world, and becoming aware at least of the endless road along which answering this cry could lead us.

It hardly needs to be said that not everyone will experience this Presence with the intensity reflected in Wordsworth's lines. Not everyone needs to experience it with such intensity. There is also what Karl Rahner refers to as 'the sober intoxication of the Spirit'.[12] For most of us, the awareness of God's presence will, presumably, be (for the most part at least) of this sober and quiet kind. It may even be of the kind which Jesus had on the cross – a very desolate, even though trusting, awareness of the presence of God. But with whatever degree of intoxication or sobriety we do experience the world as sacrament of God, we will not easily, if at all, experience 'the sacraments' as sacraments in isolation from this: without 'the mysticism of everyday life, the discovery of God in all things,'[13] there is not likely to be a mysticism of seven isolated moments in church life.

A point worth noting here is that throughout history certain experiences have been found to disclose this Presence in a particularly striking way – experiences with which we in the West of Ireland at least are very familiar. Always evocative was, for example, the awesomeness of the mountain, be it Horeb or Sinai or Tabor or the Reek. Suggestive too was the life-giving freshness of water, be it the common well-spring or the great river like the Ganges or the Jordan. The vastness, the loneliness and the barrenness of the wilderness, with whatever hungry grass it produced, brought great biblical figures in particular into contact with the silence of their being and with the distant sounds which they could hear echoed there. More, much more, than appears on the surface was perceived in the life-force experienced in the springtime. *Super*abundance seemed pointed to in the fruitfulness and harvest of autumn. To draw attention to that 'more' and to celebrate that 'superabundance', these places and seasons were celebrated in ritual: the arrival of spring was ritualised by mummers long before these were Christianised and called 'brídeogs'; mid-summer, so symbolic of light, was celebrated long before it became the feast of the Baptist; the superabundance glimpsed in autumn and in the harvest was marked by a feast of apples and nuts before this celebration became associated with the Christian feasts of all saints and all souls; Newgrange marked mid-winter before Christmas did; birth and marriage and death always evoked a sense of awe which cried out to be celebrated in ritual, and these events were in fact always surrounded by ritual.

In a world, then, which was experienced as sacramental, certain seasons and events and places were, and still can be, perceived as focusing in an unusually intense way the Presence of God, as being in a special way sacramental, in a special way 'doors to the sacred.'[14]

IV

It is, of course, in *people* above all that the 'more' begins to appear. And it is, indeed, through the insight of other people, especially those among whom we live, that each of us is helped to arrive at our own religious insight. For Christians, the 'more', with all its strangeness, appeared in a unique way in Jesus of Nazareth. It is important to remember how it appeared in him. It appeared in the way he lived and died and is experienced now as Alive, in his teaching and his loving, his touching and his healing, his vision for our world and his commitment to that vision. He, of all people, is, in the Christian experience, *the* one in whom 'there is more than appears on the surface and yet the surface is where the depth begins to appear'; *the* one uniquely laden with divine presence and power; *the* sacrament and symbol of God.

Jesus is experienced by the Christian community as being present with it and in it. But this presents a challenge. The challenge is for the Christian community, in whatever place it exists, to let Jesus, and the 'more' which appeared on the surface of his life, appear on the surface of its own life too.

In the light of the way in which the theology of the sacraments has developed, it is legitimate to think of seven broad areas of life in which the Christian community can and ought to do this – seven areas which broadly correspond to what 'the sacraments' are about. It is legitimate to think of the church as challenged to become a certain type of community – a community which is trying always to be initiating people into that new, free, uplifted and uplifting life which Jesus was able to live himself and to inspire others to live; a community which is struggling always to be a confirming, encouraging, and supportive force in the lives of people who are trying to live that authentic human life; a community characterised by the way in which it tries to share its life and break its bread for others; one which is committing itself again and again to the work of reconciling those who are alienated and hurting; one struggling to care for and to heal the wounded and the weak ones in society; one striving to hold on to, and be a sign of, the ideal of faithful love; one also always striving to stand for, by giving an experience of, the style of leadership which Jesus exercised, a servant-pastor style.

For the Christian community this will, of course, always be a matter of struggling – to recall Tennyson, the '... margin fades for ever and for ever when I move'. But the 'more' which appeared in

Jesus is so strange that it can appear at least as much *in* the struggle, as in its successful outcome. When, however, Jesus and the 'more' which he embodied, does begin to appear on the surface of the life of this community, in these ways especially, then the community itself can really be experienced by those who come into contact with it as being indeed, in its whole humble struggle, laden with divine presence and power, a door to the sacred, a sacrament of Christ and of God.

When the community itself is experienced in this way, then those acts which are generally called 'the sacraments', can also be experienced as significant events. What the community does when it performs these actions is to do, in the most official and formal way, at key-moments in the life of the individual, what really it is always striving to do – offer and strengthen new life, break and share bread, reconcile the alienated and heal the sick, commit itself to love faithfully and to lead lovingly. All this it does in 'the sacraments' in a most solemn way, with ritual and ceremony, as human needs demand. Experienced as actions of a community which in its life generally is found to be embodying Jesus, the 'more' which so graciously touched us through him, 'the sacraments', when properly celebrated, can themselves be experienced as embodiments of this graciousness – as 'outward signs of inward grace'. They can then be experienced as focusing the wider presence of Jesus and the 'more' which appeared in him – somewhat as those seasons and events and places referred to earlier can be experienced as focusing the divine presence which pervades the whole world.[15] But, isolated from this wider embodying of the 'more' and the 'depth' which touched human life in Jesus, 'the sacraments' will be experienced as very strange rituals indeed – in fact, as being like nothing on earth.

Renewal of sacramental life, which, obviously, is needed today, is more challenging than, perhaps, is often thought. It calls for more than renewal of the liturgical celebration of the sacraments and indeed for more than a new theological understanding of sacraments, basic though these are. It calls also for a renewal of our *experience* of sacraments. Today 'the sacraments' need to be experienced as symbols in which there is a focusing, not so much of some invisible substance thought of as 'grace', but of graciousness – God's graciousness, experienced by wounded ones long ago as present to them in Jesus, and willed by God to be experienced today as present through the Body of Jesus, the Christian community, especially the community in the place in which we live.

Notes:
1. *Ascending Flame, Descending Dove,*Westminster Press, 1975, p 44.
2. This phrase is attributed to Paul Tillich by Joseph Martos, *Doors to the Sacred*, SCM Press, London, p 9.
3. *A New Catechism*, Burns and Oates, London, 1969, p 17.
4. From the poem, *Ulysses.*
5. *Theological Investigations*, Vol 9, DLT, London, 1972, p 122.
6. *The Idea of the Holy*, OUP, 1958, passim.
7. In regard to seeing God in the world around us, we must, of course, distinguish between *pantheism*, which would identify God with the world, and *panentheism*, which would see everything as grounded in God and, therefore, God as being immanent in everything.
8. From the poem, *God's Grandeur.*
9. See the poem, *The Presence of God.*
10. See the poem, *Advent.*
11. cf Karl Rahner, *Theological Investigations*, Vol 4, DLT, London, 1966, p 108.
12. Karl Rahner, *The Spirit in the Church*, Burns and Oates, London, 1979, p 22.
13. *The Spirit in the Church*, p 22.
14. Joseph Martos, *Doors to the Sacred*, p 16. Note the account here of Mircea Eliade's analysis of 'how sacramental rites and objects function in a variety of religions and cultures from the most ancient to the most contemporary.' – pp 15ff.
15. See John Macquarrie's use of the word 'focus' in, for example, the context of miracles, *Principles of Christian Theology* (Revised Edition) SCM Press, London, 1977, pp 253ff: 'The miracle focuses the presence and action that underlies the whole and makes sense of the whole.' Also in the context of christology, pp 300ff.

Woman of Faith
Augustine Valkenburg

One of the earliest stories I remember hearing in Ballinrobe, Co. Mayo, was about Mary, the Mother of God, as she walked the road on a wet stormy evening with her child in her arms. It was blowing so mightily that it took all her strength to keep the shawl wrapped around Our Saviour. Well she continued on until they came to a forge on the right side of the road as you come in to the town. (To interrupt the story for a moment. It never seemed to occur to any one of us to ask how it came about that the Blessed Virgin happened to be walking on the Carrownalecka road!) Inside, the smith was blowing the big bellows. The sparks flew up from the glowing flame at the heart of the coke fire. Our Lady wished God's blessing on the work, and asked if the smith would make a breast pin for her to hold the shawl around herself and her child. 'That I'll do with pleasure, good woman', said the smith. 'Why wouldn't I? Come in out of the rain and dry yourself and the child by the fire.' He drew up a stool beside the fire for her and began to make the pin. It wasn't long it took him. He fixed the pin on the shawl for her before she set out. The Blessed Virgin left him her blessing and asked God that the smith would never be out of work.

That is the story. And here it is in Irish, to show you how much is lost in translation:

Bhí Máthair Dé ag siúl roimpi le titim na h-oíche uair. Ní hé amháin go raibh sé ag báisteach ach bhí an ghaoth ag séideadh an tseáil a bhí thart uirthi féin agus ar ár Slánaitheoir. Bhí an bheirt acu báite fliuch. Shiúil sí lei riamh go dtáinig sí go cearta. Bhí gabha istigh ag séideadh na mbolg agus bhí an tine in aon chaor amháin aige. Chuir an Mhaighdean Bheannaithe bail ó Dhia ar an obair, gur iarr air an ndéanfadh sé bioran di a choinneodh a seál uirthi féin 's a Páiste. 'Déanfad agus fáilte, a bhean chóir,' arsan gabha. 'Tuige nach ndéanfainn? Gabh isteach ón mbáistigh agus triomaigh thú féin agus an leanbh, an fhaid agus a bheas mé á dhéanamh.' Níorbh fhada go raibh an biorán déanta aige. É féin a ghreamaigh an seál leis an mbiorán di nuair a bhí sí réidh le imeacht. D'fhág an Mhaighdean Bheannaithe a beannacht aige 's d'iarr ar Dhia nach mbeadh sé gan obair choíche.

There are many similar stories in Irish folklore as indeed there are in the folk traditions of all the Christian countries. Some when fashioned by master-craftsmen like Felix Timmermans, become classics. In his *Het Kindekin Jesus in Vlaanderen*[1] we accompany the Holy Family to and from Nazareth through a landscape that is timeless but which merges imperceptibly into the Flemish countryside. What strikes one most forcibly in all these stories is the assimilation of the unearthly to the earthly; the heavenly mingles easily, almost casually with the terrestrial. This should not surprise us. The storyteller is on the Faith, and his stories are for those who believe. For them the Incarnation is an abiding reality – the wonder of wonders to be accepted in faith and gratitude. 'The Word was made flesh and dwelt amongst us.' Neither Jesus nor his Blessed Mother, nor St Joseph for that matter, are bound in time or space. It is quite natural then that they would walk a *bóithrín* in Mayo if they wished. That being so, the candle must be placed in the window at Christmas to light the Holy Family home. That candle is a Light too for Padraig, for Bridie and for all the young ones who have made it to Euston Station or latterly to Luton Airport in order to be home for Christmas. The Catholic tradition discovers Christ in the world, not in the abstract logic of revelation, but as a warm personal presence. And this happens only when Mary is also present at the background of consciousness. It is Mary who makes Christ fully human by making a home for him. Without her he would be homeless on earth. That is the way God wanted it to be.

The Christ Child in Flanders

Mary's personal pilgrimage of faith began with the annunciation. (Lk 1:26-38) A redeemed person like us, although perfectly redeemed from the first moment of her existence, Mary too had to live by faith. Her faith, though never weakened by sin, was nevertheless like our faith. It had to be lived out when the way was dark and full of pain.

The word of God came to Mary of Nazareth. The angel Gabriel said to her, 'Hail full of grace.' In Luke's Greek: *Chaire, kecharitomene* – rejoice O highly favoured one. Interestingly it was not the appearance of the angel that worried Mary. The angel still bothers people. He does not, of course, bother those who do not believe in angels, they simply reject them out of hand. What greatly disturbed Mary was the angel's greeting. How often it is like this when God intervenes in a human life, when the unexpected and the impossible happen. And the first reaction to that kind of intervention is often one of fear: it can grip, almost paralyse. What is needed is a reassuring word or gesture, a healing word. 'Do not be afraid, Mary, you have won God's favour.' That word of divine love, for such it is, has a unique quality. It not only reassures, it liberates, gives life, inspires.

Gabriel did not greet her first by her proper, earthly name, Mary, but by this new name, 'highly favoured one'. What does this name mean? The phrase that follows, 'the Lord is with you', was an immeasurable compliment. Our Irish greeting, *Dia dhuit*, and the phrase at parting, *Beannacht Dé leat*, are prayers, good wishes. But

Gabriel was not expressing a wish that God might be with Mary. He was stating as a fact that God was with her. There is no record of its ever having been addressed to anyone else. Mary's Son was to promise to be with his Church until the end of time. But as we know, and Gabriel knew, but as Mary did not yet know, the greeting was to have a meaning for Mary which it never had for a human being before, and never could again. The word of God came to Mary of Nazareth. Her immediate response to that word, is not as we are sometimes told, to say Yes to God, but to ask questions. First of all she wants to know. How shall these things be? Mary needs to know if she is to be able to respond appropriately to what is asked of her. She has to go through that process of discovering God's will which we normally have to undertake. Most decisions involve reflection, consideration, working through things and working them out. This does not mean that you have to see your whole life as one interminable series of world-shaking decisions. We can well see our life, too, as the slow and steady unfolding of God's will within us. But even then there may have to be drastic measures from time to time. God may require some major change of direction, some breakthrough or breakout, perhaps at the onset of middle age or on retirement from a particular job. It may well be that Mary's life had its crisis moments: the annunciation, the cross, Pentecost. But whether your life seems mainly a matter of decisions, or primarily a process of growth, in either case you must have discernment if the life of God is going to deepen within you. 'Lord, teach me your ways; Lord, let me know your paths', was the prayer of the psalmist. His ways enter each of our lives; his paths lie through our hearts and not simply across the wider stage of world history or the history of salvation.

But to discern those ways presupposes a thorough Christian faith. You cannot build up a practice of the discernment of God's will working in your life unless you accept the basic presuppositions of the Jewish-Christian tradition concerning God and his activity. First, God is a God who acts, and who acts recognisably as God. Second, his activity is not monochrome, uniform. He comes in special ways as well as universally. He comes into the lives of each directly, whether spectacularly or by the gentlest of touches. He requires distinctive things from different people, as he required something so distinctive from Mary. I cannot tell what God will want of me simply from looking at what he has asked of people in general. How can I acquire this sense of what God wants from me? Here the commonplace institutional mesh of our lives, the day to day existence of the Church, may sieve that will through to us. We live within a Church which offers a tradition of teaching about Christian living. We live in particular communities within the

Church, parishes, monasteries, schools, families, and these are structured by people with various jobs and responsibilities. We can use sound common sense about the divine implications of where we are placed humanly in life, not the common sense of Mr Worldly-wise, but a common sense formed by the gospel and the tradition of the Church.

Zachary, the father of John the Baptist, when told of a son to be conceived, was incredulous and asked the angel for a sign. Mary was not incredulous, she asked for no signs. She simply asked, 'How can this come about since I am a virgin?' Gabriel answered. 'The Holy Spirit will come upon you, and the power of the Most High will cover you with its shadow. And so the child will be holy and will be called Son of God.' Mary's question was answered. The child was not to be conceived as she herself had been conceived, in the usual way of marriage. That which, in any conception, is provided by the mother, she would provide. But what in every other conception the father provided would in this one case be produced by a miracle of God's plan. To accept that, faith was, and still is, a prime requisite.

God speaks to the soul who is open and feels the need of God. Like the merchant in the parable, on the look-out for fine pearls, you know you have found the truly precious pearl by the joy it produces. Sometimes the person who finds the treasure has no doubt, and the joy is instantaneous; sometimes long and laborious tests alone will prove the worth of it. But always the joy. So Mary, having questioned the angel to find out all she needs to know, says, 'Behold the handmaid of the Lord. Be it done unto me according to your word.' She could so easily have responded by that fatalistic Middle Eastern acceptance of the declared will of God, *Inshallagh*: it is God's will. What a bleak phrase that can be! It is certainly not Mary's attitude. *Genoito moi*: may it be done to me. This is Mary's 'Yes' to God, spoken by a girl in her teens from an insignificant townlet in Galilee, bride of a carpenter. Luke gives us our strongest New Testament evidence for the massively important fact that Mary was a disciple of Jesus. In consenting to become the mother of God, Mary was not just the mouthpiece of the Holy Spirit speaking through her. She was a free and responsible woman who knew what was being proposed to her and was prepared to accept the consequences of her response. These would include the consternation of Joseph, the man to whom Mary was espoused, and there would be the wagging tongues of the village gossips. But this was Mary's act of faith. She acted out of her freedom and integrity as a person and a daughter of God. To choose what is better means a real detachment from our own preferences. The point of selling all you have, of all living that costs and that hurts, lies not in the pain of loss but in the joy in the kingdom. 'My spirit rejoices in God my Saviour.' It is only when we give up what we love for the joy of what we have found that we are truly close to the kingdom of heaven. That was Mary's discovery at the annunciation.

The gospel picture we have of Mary is lit up with her loving concern for others. From the very start, at the crucial moment of the annunciation, you see it. When the angel left her, you would expect to read: 'Mary treasured all these things and pondered them in her heart.' But Luke does not have that well-known verse here. Instead Mary rose and went 'with haste' to visit her cousin Elizabeth, to be of help to her. We tend to think of the visitation (Lk 1: 40-56) as a meeting of two mothers. But far more important was the meeting of the two sons. Could it be for this that Mary went in such great haste? At her words of greeting Elizabeth is filled with the Holy Spirit and exclaims, 'You are blessed among women ... and blessed is she who believed.' This is Elizabeth's confession of faith in the incarnation and in the holiness of Mary. 'Why should I be honoured with a visit from the mother of my Lord?' Every Christian who has a living faith will marvel all his life long, in both the knowing and the unknowing of faith, that such a thing could have happened to him. The Spirit also showed Elizabeth very palpably how it is that, in this cousin whom she knows so well, the mother of her Lord comes to her. 'For the moment your greeting reached my ears the child in my womb leaped for joy.' It is through her own child that she realises how blessed Mary's child is, and that it is Mary and not herself who is blessed because 'she believed that the promise made to her by the Lord would be fulfilled.'

Elizabeth's happiness and accord are aroused by her child's mission and joy. What better thing could happen to her than that her child, the next generation, should come to salvation? This is a mentality which can be seen as summarising the whole New Testament: to be blessed in one's children. It has relevance for our day and our country. Prayer is the voice of faith. It is the dearest wish of parents to hand on the faith and to see their children make their own of it. But faith needs nourishment, particularly in the 'domestic church', the family. In the past the majority of people were deprived of a reading knowledge of their own language, so that spiritual reading, the Bible if it were available, was denied them. There is less excuse today for the neglect of spiritual reading and for the almost total absence of Bible-study groups. In the very skillful delineation of the four missions (of Jesus and Mary, of John and Elizabeth) we recognise the active presence of the Holy Spirit. The fact that Elizabeth prays the words of the Hail Mary 'in a loud voice' is, as always in the Bible, the sign that God is speaking through her mouth. The whole scene is one single inspiration containing multiple articulations. It is also the scene contemplated in the second joyful mystery of the Rosary of the Blessed Virgin Mary.

It is important to emphasise the influence of the Rosary in forming the life of faith. The daily praying and meditating on the mysteries of Christ's life in union with his mother – and in reference to the Mass – moulded communities, despite human failings, into fervent Christian communities to whom it came natural to see God in all things. The devotion was preached widely by the Dominicans. Their four priories in county Mayo – Urlar, Strade, Rathfran and Burrishoole – served as bases from which the parish missions were preached. By the sixteenth century the Rosary was well settled in Ireland, and then, with the Mass proscribed, it became even more prominent in the lives of the people. The beads along with the crucifix became the symbols of the faith. The prayers that clustered around the Rosary reveal the soul of a sensitive, caring people who kept in mind the needs of the whole Church, indeed all humankind, living and dead. Here is a typical Offering of the Rosary:

> We offer up this Rosary in honour of and in the name of Jesus and in honour of the glorious Virgin Mary to share in the holy sacrifice of the Mass, with the same intention for which our Saviour offered himself on the tree of the cross for our sake ... for every poor soul especially our own poor dead ones. If they were guilty of negligence in confession or forgetfulness of Mass, may their pains be lessened, their glory increased. May the unbelievers of the world be converted to the right state. May God not permit us a premature death or a sudden death, but a good and holy death in the state of grace, death after anointing and repentance ... May the holy Body of the Lord be our poor soul's eternal provision on leaving this world, and Mary's protecting mantle be spread over us. May God grant that to us.

It is the prayer of a people, not clerical; people of the Hidden Ireland who were poor and deprived, but rich in faith and in kinship with him who knew pain and heartbreak.

During 'the hidden life' of Jesus at Nazareth, Mary's life was hidden too 'with Christ in God' (Col 3:5) in faith. The child to whom she gave 'the name Jesus' would have been called by the Aramaic equivalent of *Íosagán*. But always Mary was conscious of the fact that her child had been called by the angel 'Son of the Most High.' She is in contact with the truth about her son only in faith and through faith. There is a deep poignancy in Mary's words to the twelve-year old lost for three days, 'My child, why have you done this to us?' (Lk 2:48) His reply, the first recorded words of Jesus, are literally out of Mary's world, 'Did you not know that I had to be about my Father's business?' He cannot spare her this pain. What he does is to make manifest his truth: he is the Son of God, comparable to no one else, and the son of a virginal mother. Luke goes on to say, 'they did not understand what he meant.' But Jesus 'went down with them and came to Nazareth and was subject to them.' He is no emancipated youth who takes on a job in opposition to his parents, who do not understand him. We would like to know much more, but the gospels present not a biography of Mary and Joseph, but the history of salvation of Christ Jesus. The infancy narrative closes with the 'signature' of its ultimate author, 'His mother kept all these things carefully in her heart.'

As the messianic mission of her song grew clearer to Mary, she as a mother became ever more open to a new dimension of her motherhood. This is very clear at the wedding feast in Cana. At first glance the incident seems to be of little importance, touching on just one aspect of human need. Mary knew that her son could in some way help the young couple. Remember he had not yet worked any miracle. As his mother, Mary felt she could make an effective appeal to her son. The perplexing reply of Jesus seems to be on an entirely different level, 'What would you have me do, woman? My hour has not yet come.' (Jn 2:4) Jesus sees Mary here more as woman than as mother. But Mary is not rebuffed by what appears to be a refusal and makes appeal to all that is profound in the heart and mission of Jesus who was sent 'to bring good news to the poor.' (Is 61:16) Her woman's heart tells her that God who created woman cannot but have a heart full of tenderness. At Cana Mary's faith in Jesus evokes his first 'sign' and helps to kindle the faith of his disciples.

The mother of our Saviour was from the very first what the world calls a self-sacrificing mother. With the annunciation Mary was the first to receive Christ's body within her, the first to 'communicate'. She must have known a thousand times better than we that she was not receiving him for her own sake, that she could never have him to herself, because he could never belong to himself. Even during Jesus' childhood, he was not hers. It was not she who taught him to be a son, but he who taught her to be a mother, and a daughter. This perfecting of Mary's faith and love is very striking in the gospel narratives. Only one evangelist mentions Mary standing at the foot of the cross and her bond with the beloved disciple, and only one reports, almost incidentally, the fact that she was present at the prayer of the church, the first Pentecost. The relationship between son and mother remains veiled, not least by his seeming rejection of her. The woman in the crowd who praised Mary, 'Blessed is the womb that bore you and the breasts that nursed you' (Lk 11:28) sensed something of the hidden mystery: from the person of the son she recognised the nature of the mother. But even here the son draws the veil by universalising this praise to all anonymous persons in the church who imitate his Mother. 'Yes, they are surely blessed who hear God's word and keep it.' There are commentators who would soften the harshness of these episodes, mistakenly. Jesus knew he could ask this of Mary, that he had her unquestioning fidelity. In short he dared not to explain, not to soften, not to smooth things over. We can be most abrupt with those we love most. When Jesus looked at Mary he knew, without her having to say a word, that she believed. That certainly was his greatest joy and consolation in life. The silence of the gospel about their relationship, far from being disturbing, is the most outstanding honour that could be paid to her.

It was at the foot of the cross that Mary became totally a mother, because it was there that she accepted the most perfectly to give everything. She gave back to the Father the dearest thing she had, and, in the same gesture, gave him to the world. All the 'privileges' she had received had been to lead up to that great fiat. It is not of great moment that the insight into these cannot be traced back to the very earliest Christian centuries: thorough reflection on revelation and its deeper implications requires a certain space of time. In giving Mary into the care of St John, Jesus provided for his widowed mother, soon to be left alone in the world, with no family and no security. But at a deeper level Jesus called Mary to a new vocation as mother of all who would come to believe in him, all his disciples. The maternal nature of Mary speaks to the hearts of people everywhere. This truth was brought home to me vividly through observing Muslim reverence for Mary: the sight of black chaddor-clad women entering the Dominican church in Tehran to light a candle before the ikon of the virgin Mariam, 'mother of a great prophet.'

Mary's love should lead us to a deeper appreciation of God's love, which is infinitely greater. 'Does a woman forget her baby at the breast, or fail to cherish the child of her womb? Yet even if she should forget, I will never forget you.' (Is 59:15) God is neither male nor female, but all that is truly human, both masculine and feminine, has its origin in God. Mary helps us to appreciate the 'feminine' side of the divine nature. She reveals the maternal face of God.

At the end, or rather at the beginning, when the pilgrim church on earth began its journey of faith at Pentecost, Mary was present among the apostles. 'All these joined in continuous prayer, together with several women, including Mary the mother of Jesus.' (Acts 1:14) Like the humanity of Christ of which it is an extension, the church is 'conceived by the Holy Spirit.' Pentecost is a continuation of the incarnation. The historical incarnation is the vital point, but it would not by itself have been enough to save humankind. We need a continuing incarnation, for only God can teach us to love. And Mary is the creature who loved God best. After Pentecost she disappears altogether. Yet we know more about her than about any other woman in sacred scripture. But what is revealed about her is shown to us for her son's sake in order to make plain the nature of the son and the way of following him.

Knowledge of Christ leads us to bless his mother, in the form of special veneration for the *Theotokos*, the God-bearer. Knowledge of Christ will help us to evaluate without prejudice the words of St Paul. 'There is one mediator between God and men, the man Jesus Christ.' (1 Tim 2:5) Knowledge of Mary shows us that her maternal care of mankind in no way diminishes the unique mediation of her son. For all her titles, she is raised up precisely as the lowly one. Her motherhood precedes and is greater than the priesthood. She is called queen of apostles because she committed herself to the work of her son, the church, more deeply, earlier and more thoroughly than they. Being men, the apostles and their successors only held an office in the church; but Mary, being a woman, represents the whole church to the church's Lord and bridegroom.

In his encyclical **Redemptoris Mater**, Pope John Paul II speaks of 'those special places where the people of God seek to meet the mother of God.' For Mayo people that rendezvous is *Cnoc Mhuire*, Knock. To kneel and give thanks to God was the first reaction of the men, women and children who saw Our Lady there on the 21st August, 1879. She was a light in their lives, a sight for sore eyes, and the rain that drenched them was disregarded for the joy of seeing Our Lady. In that year Mayo was in dire straits – potato blight, famine, typhus fever. Those who could emigrate did.

Writing from Melbourne to Ballinrobe, Christmas 1879, a young emigrant asked his mother a poignant question, 'Is it true the Blessed Virgin appeared at Knock?' A century later, October 1979, the great-granddaughter of that mother wrote in a letter to Iran, 'By the time the papal helicopter came into sight, the hillside was black with people and the hills beyond rising black too. I kept thinking of the Famine for some reason: that and then this. Like mushrooms that you think are gone forever and there they rise again. And you know how we feel about mushrooms, delight and discovery. Tears poured down all round; men too but no great shouting. It seemed enough up on the hillside, to be there.'

Mary is a real person, living in the present – not an historical personage who lived for a time, only to become a faint memory in the pages of history. Although we relate to her now living gloriously in heaven, she is still the same person we find in the gospels, a woman of faith, strong and courageous, a wife and mother, going out to others (Visitation), concerned for their welfare (Cana), steadfast in suffering (Calvary). She is and has always been close to those who confided themselves to her loving care and asked her intercession with Almighty God.

Those who belong to Mayo have a habit of doing just that, however vagrant their course. I am thinking of one now, born six miles or so from Knock. Like many of us he spent his early years in the sister county of Galway, not in acquiring knowledge but in making music and poetry. They were kind to him there. Why not? A Conamara man told me. *As Contae Mhuigheo a fhaighmid na sagairt agus na tincéirí* ...

Antoine Raifteirí loved Mary; his sightless eyes saw her, his heart sang to her more tunefully than the old fiddle. For the blind poet, Mary was 'Queen of paradise, mother and maid, mirror of grace, queen of angels and saints. Protect me, Mary, and I'll be safe'.

A Bhanríon phárthais, máthair 's maighdean,
Scathán na ngrás, aingeal 's naomh,
Cuirim cosaint m'anama ar do láimh,
A Mhuire, na diúltaigh mé, 's beidh mé saor.

These lines could well be inscribed on the walls of the basilica, for Raifteirí would dearly have loved to welcome her to Knock. But Mary anticipted her client and welcomed him home in the winter of 1835, on Christmas Day.

A Lost Tradition?

Leon Ó Mórcháin

In the Belderg valley, near Ballycastle in North Mayo, recent excavations have unearthed evidence of ancient farming believed to date from 3,000-3,500 B.C. Already the site is becoming internationally famous; preserved, protected and sign-posted so that the modern visitor may see and wonder at the Neolithic methods of cultivation by the revealed landscape and artefacts uncovered by Dr Seamus Caulfield and his team. The whole project presents a literal revelation, one which will interest not only the professional archaeologist but anyone who is curious about how people lived in earlier times. The site should have a very special interest, laced with a *mórtas cine*, for the present generation which inhabits all the adjacent area of Mayo. Evidence of ancient ridges, plough-marks, grinding-querns and a possible granary have been discovered as the layers of bog were removed – a blanket bog which apparently grew at a very rapid rate about the year 1,000 B.C. and effectively sealed off that part of our ancient past.

I have a proposition which is analogous. In short it is this: that there is another excavation which we could make. We could, with the implements at hand, uncover another, more elusive scenario, namely, the thinking, attitudes, beliefs, philosophy and spirituality of our same ancestors, and be at least equally fascinated by how all these were expressed in their lives. A whole spiritual panorama has been engulfed and lost to us. Because these spiritual bounties cannot be seen and handled as can the artefacts now in Belderg, they may appear less exciting to an unthinking mind. However, whereas the implements and even the methods of Neolithic farmers can add little if anything to our present-day husbandry, the treasures of which I speak, being spiritual, are more resistant and enduring. They have an energy that resists being smothered, and could indeed enliven and enrich the way that we understand spirituality today. Spirituality has at least two meanings: one which refers to things that are just immaterial – like beauty, poetry, thought, dignity or art; and the other, which refers to things that are more specifically religious – such as prayer, virtue, grace, the sacraments, or truth. These two meanings often overlap but in this article I intend to focus on that second meaning. And at the obvious risk of appearing didactic I shall repeatedly imply that in our age a concerted effort should be made to roll back the avalanche and to allow the indigenous religious fauna to breathe and flower again. The picture I paint is, of course, common to the whole island of Ireland: Mayo must not appropriate it to itself. Equally however, it must be of concern to every thinking Mayo person that, despite some recent efforts to revive our traditional Irish spirituality, little enough of that tradition seems to inform our minds and our lives.

What tradition? To address that question it is necessary to describe, in however sketchy strokes, the kind of Ireland into which Christianity was introduced in the fifth century of Our Lord. That society was predominantly Celtic, descendant of the warrior Celts who had come to Ireland from Spain (or Africa? or India?) some thousand years before. They were cousins of the Gauls whom Caesar in his war commentaries described as much given to religion; kinsmen of Saint Paul's 'little children', the 'senseless' Galatians. Even as a yardstick by which to judge the perceived image of the Irish today, it is of interest to list some of the attested characteristics of these early progenitors. The Celts were known to be eloquent, foolishly brave, volatile, nature-loving, other-worldly (and in that sense very religious), warm and argumentative. By the arrival of Christianity in Ireland they had developed a full-blown culture, particularly advanced in laws, religion and education. Patrick and his co-missionaries did not try to uproot that established culture: rather they accepted it and used it as the stock onto which they grafted their Christian message. As might be expected then, the breed or nature of that old stock was to imbue and flavour the new shoot; just as indeed it would give it a life-energy and cause it to flower. And that particular flower, which I describe loosely here as 'traditional Irish spirituality' retains recognisable strains of the parent Celtic culture and religion in the cultivar which has been produced over a millenium and a half. The traditional Irish spirituality of which I speak has most of the following main traits: otherworldliness, a warm and intimate devotion to Christ in his passion, a love of scripture, a close relationship with Our Blessed Lady, a reverence for the Eucharist based on a real faith, a gift of prayer, an appreciation of penance and fasting, a community spirit based on the Body of Christ, a consequent reverence for the dead, and a closeness to nature as a link with the Creator. Even in the limited space available here it will be necessary to examine some of those traits to see how they surfaced in the lives and lifestyle of Irish people.

The Irish trait of other-worldliness (and many observers have recognised this even in the Irish character today) was a Celtic gift of gliding easily between two worlds. The Celts had their gods, of course; prominent among them the god of the harvest, Lugh, to whose festival of Lúnasa we can directly trace the Croagh Patrick pilgrimage both in place and in time of year. The Celts had a worship of Earth as mother. It is tempting to see a relic of this worship in the traditional Irish love of land; or again in the deep-felt resentment to violation of the environment which has very recently shown itself in Mayo. And the Celts and their descendants believed in their own version of Utopia or land of never-never-Hy-brasil or Tír na nÓg. It is almost too easy to see the Christian parallels; and interesting, too, to notice how these strands lived on in the typical Irish beliefs in fairies, leprechauns, ghosts as well as in the remarkable Irish Catholic reverence for the dead, for anniversary Masses and for November devotion, which retains vestiges of the closeness and almost the presence of the dead which the Celts believed in during their ancient feast of Samhain. In fine, the traditional Irish mind had 'an equal feeling of at-homeness with this world and the world beyond' and this appears over the whole spectrum of Irish written sources whether in the Fiannaíocht tales, the writings of the earliest Irish monks, the medieval poets and down to Yeats or even Kavanagh. Perhaps particularly Kavanagh.

An extra-ordinary aspect of Irish spirituality is the intimacy, informed as well as informal, with which people related to the person who was being adored or honoured. To use an Irishism, they 'made bold' on their deity and on their saints. The Irish praying mind even today dispenses with titles: it is not 'Saint' this-or-that; it is simply and familiarly 'Dóchas linn, a Phádraic' and 'A Mhíchil, a aingeal uasail' and 'A Bhríd, a Mhuire na nGael.' To the initiated this might well sound syrupy or boorishly over-weening: it is as likely to be misappreciated as our own familiar use of 'Tomeen' or 'Séamusheen'. It is in fact a recurring freature of the Irish way of thinking in prayer, a kind of reverent irreverence in pushing the door of language across the threshold of the sacred. And it did not stop with addressing the ordinary saints. In an early hymn to the infant Jesus, probably by Saint Íde, she first uses the truly untranslatable term 'Íosagán' (almost, as it were, 'little Jesuseen') which like many more revealing and heart-felt expressions runs the risk of derision as soon as it is expressed openly. An old poem of the seventh century written by Blathmac, sympathises with Mary:

> Come to me, loving Mary
> that I may caoin with you your darling son..

And in authentic continuation with that sentiment Máirtín Ó Direáin of Aran wrote in 1942 his invitation to Mary to spend Christmas on the island:

> Beidh coinnle geala i ngach fuinneog lasta
> Is tine móna ar theallach adhainte

The thread goes through the whole Irish life-pattern. It shows in a medieval Munster Communion poem: 'A Íosa, a mhuirnín dílis, ní suíochán duit mo theanga' as it does in Sean O'Casey's line in *Juno and the Paycock:* 'Blessed Virgin where were you when me darlin' son was riddled with bullets!'; or in Chesterton's recorded line from a Dublin woman during Congress week in 1932: 'Well, if it rains now, He'll have brought it on Himself.' Two further example of this kind of daring informality in prayer have always impressed me, probably because they are both from Mayo. One is the testimony of Brigid Trench, the oldest witness of the Apparition at Knock in 1879. Brigid's story (but as we shall see, not her exact story) goes: 'I threw myself on my knees and ... I went in immediately to kiss, as I thought, the feet of the Blessed Virgin, but I felt nothing in the embrace but the wall.' And the other example is the recorded story of the touching expressions, used half-aloud, by a Claremorris lady as she 'did' the Stations of the Cross in the parish church there some fifty years ago. At the station of the third fall poor Lily Gallagher always sighed aloud: 'Jesus, yer down again!' And at the stripping of the garments, 'Ah, if the Gollaher's were there, it wouldn't happen to you!' Smile, of course we do; but in the ending of our smiles I always find that there is a silence. Perhaps it is still that 'at-homeness with this world and the world beyond'.

The all-importance of the Eucharist (as sacrifice and sacrament) in Irish spirituality has been well recorded, and, despite the changing attitudes of modern decades, is still attested to in great measure by statistics as well as by simple observation. The oft-quoted reply of Augustine Birrell in 1905 (when he conducted a survey to ascertain why Ireland had never accepted the Reformed religion) was: 'It is the Mass that matters.' The reply was Caiaphas-like in its unconscious truth. The story of the Mass in Ireland is so well recorded that I shall not dwell on it here. It runs a connecting pole through the curtain-rings of the centuries of Irish church history: it picks up Aughagower and Muigheo na Sacsan; it picks up the Reek and the Mass-rocks; it picks up the scores of abbeys from Murrisk to Ballyhaunis, from Cong to Ballintubber; it links the station-house and the Sunday-clothes and the shrine at Knock. And all along there was the draught of human intimacy spiked with faith. On a morning in the eighteen-nineties Father William Joyce, parish priest of Louisburgh, walked to a station-house in Caher to the home of a family with whom he had recently had a great quarrel. He was met at the door by the parents and with the welcome: 'Not only for yourself, Father, but for the One you're bringing with you.' Surely it is permissible to see this as the echo of the great acclamation after the Consecration at the mass-rocks: 'Céad míle fáilte romhat, a Thiarna!', an acclamation which unfortunately, the Irish representatives at Vatican II did not remember when they were successful in having an exception made (for Ireland!) to use an alternative response: 'My Lord and My God!'

Flowing from, and to, that understanding and appreciation of Eucharist was the traditional sense of community, of *pobal Dé*. (Another term which was presented to us as novel from the Second Vatican Council, when we had almost forgotten that for centuries, and even today in Gaeltacht areas, our Irish priests addressed their congregations as 'A phobail Dé') The ideal was translated into practice by the custom of neighbourliness, of the visiting-house, of the *meitheal*, of *ar scáth a chéile a mhaireas na daoine*. Close to the understanding of the Mass was the empathy with the Passion and death of Christ and the related sympathy with Mary as with a bereaved neighbour. These, in turn, though they did take the liberty that we associate with forklore, were fed off an enlightened knowledge of the sacred word; a study which is still witnessed to by such treasures as the Book of Kells and its less illustrious companions (invariably copies of some part of the inspired word) as well as the many biblical high crosses of which that at Clonmacnoise is probably the most well known. Naturally this overflowed into the people's private lives. Perhaps it was the placing of the Crucifixion into the human tragedy of their own experience of death and the intimacy (again!) of their joining Mary in a *caoineadh* for the dead. The well-known (or is it?) *caoineadh* hymn, *Caoineadh na dTrí Muire*, speaks within elbow distance of the sorrowing Mother:

'An é sin an maicín a d'iompar mé trí ráithe?
Ochón agus ochón ó!'
'Ó éist a mháithrín agus ná goil go cráite!
Ochón agus ochón ó'

Again it was in the simple reaction to a domestic minor tragedy, a cut knee or a wounded hand: 'Ba mhó páis Chríost ná é', or in the pregnant Easter wish to a neighbour: 'Toradh na páise agat!' So, for all its informality and intimacy, our people's language fashioned a way of oftentimes expressing a condensed theological truth. Frequently this was done with an economy of language – a *comhgar cainte* – whose compact wisdom is so evident in the hundreds of Irish seanfhocail. So Christ became known simply as Mac Dé: or more incarnationally as Mac Mhuire. The rich burden of such terms will easily escape a mind unfamiliar with the Irish rural practice of adding to a person's name, for identification, the name of a parent (in a genitive case). Of their myriad epithets for Our Blessed Lady the most frequently used by far was the theological one, Máthair Dé. (It is tempting to imagine, though it can hardly be proved, that that basic title was introduced into the infant Irish church as a direct influence of the Council of Ephesus in 341),

For a people whose prayer-life was sustained by such an insight into the basics of religion, it is hardly to be wondered at that a sizeable collection of folk-prayers has survived, at least in their written form. Little wonder, too, that they undertook the practice of penance. What is, however, wonder-ful is the quality and the quantity of the prayers that are still available. One wonders less if one goes back to what must surely be the written fount of all our Irish Christian spirituality, the *Faoistín Phádraic*, and sample there the true man of prayer. And indeed of penance, although one feels that his spiritual successors in this mission-field even out-did him in penance from time to time! A few centuries after Patrick's time, in the middle of the eighth century to be exact, there was founded at Tallaght a movement which really deserves more attention than is being given either in the spiritual or educational training of Ireland's people. The movement was the *Céilí Dé* or 'Servants of God' and it brought into flower an almost unique kind of spirituality which was soundly based on a love of the Creator through loving appreciation of, and spiritual union with, his creation, especially as presented in nature. For them, natural and supernatural were one continuum. It was of these *Céilí Dé* that Robin Flower, author of the classic, *The Irish Tradition*, wrote: 'it was because they brought into (their) environment an eye washed miraculously clean by a continual spiritual exercise, that they, the first in Europe, had that strange vision of natural things in an almost un-natural purity'. The founder of the *Céilí Dé Maelrúin*, must surely be the patron saint of all environment groups!

So how and when did this magnificence disappear? Before we look for an answer to that question, it will be well to have two facts established. One fact is that the Irish were a race of human beings with human faults, too. To remember and parade all the spiritual achievements of our people is by no means to deny that they had a complement of faults and human deficiencies like the people of other countries. It is because this article advocates a revival that it chooses not to list the aspects of the seamier side! The balancing fact is that the Irish people as a whole did create the kind of culture that I describe. And that, for all the modern puerile cynicism about 'the island of saints and scholars', the fact is that this island was once widely known by that name, and, as far as can be judged by human knowledge, merited it. It disappeared because, like the farms at Belderg, it was smothered and entombed. Strangely, the 'avalanche' did not happen during the penal ages. Predictably, the contrary happened: adversity reinforced a persecuted people and made them even more tenacious. All the intervening centuries of ruined abbeys, of continental colleges, of the *paidrín páirteach*, of mass-rocks, of outlawed *sagart a rún* and, in our own county, of *sean na Sagart*, had left few lasting negative marks. Rather it was in the century of emancipation – the nineteenth – that the landslide gradually but inexorably all but stifled a Christian culture. And the reason that this historical fact has attracted, as I think, insufficient attention is that when the old culture was being smothered, it was by the introduction of another, different, Christian culture which in the greater part of Ireland is the dominant one today.

In an article in *The Furrow* (December 1954) called 'The Integral Irish Tradition', An tAthair Donnchadh Ó Floinn, then Irish professor at Maynooth, drew attention to this fact of history with an expressed wish 'to repair this century-old oversight by making the Irish church today enter into conscious communion with the Irish church of old.' His thesis was that on being at last emancipated (1829) the Irish church, through its leaders, lost the great opportunity of regaining consciousness of its past and rebuilding on traditions such as those to which I have earlier referred. The Irish church, he said, 'had forgotten how to fashion beautiful tools for divine worship; how to compose hymns for her children to sing aloud ... So she made common cause with her sister church in England, and ... accepted the tutelage of the younger sister, learning from her how to build, and pray, and preach, and sing Father Faber's *Faith of our Fathers.*' The Celtic strain of Christianity had been nurtured here for nearly fourteen hundred years by 1829. The graft had 'taken'. It was foolhardy in the extreme and even monstrous that on arriving at freedom we should disown this ancient growth and try to supplant it with a cultivar that was strange and other. It was against nature. And this is in truth what happened in the nineteenth century in Ireland. Roots were suppressed, even unearthed, in a general (and genuine) quest for progress, education, civilisation – and religion!

It was a strange century in Ireland. Even the bitter and bigoted sectarianism and inter-church rivalry of the latter half of the century (a sad, sad era for Christianity which was highlighted in Mayo because of the 'colonies' in Louisburgh and in Achill) did not make Irish Catholic church leaders pause and check a compass. The Reformed church came to be known as the 'Teampall Gallda' by use of an equation which said that English was Protestant and Protestant was English. (One recalls from the Louisburgh of the thirties hearing the unusual number-plates of English cars being referred to as 'Protestant numbers'!) Still, curiously, despite that assumed dichotomy, the Irish Catholic Church, as Ó Floinn points out, was taking its English counterpart as pattern! Not that it should be in any way imagined that Irish Christian spirituality became the sole preserve of the Catholic church here. For instance, as is easily seen on reflection, it was in the Church of Ireland that the great scriptural tradition of Kells, Tallaght, the Faoistín etc., was best maintained. The welcome Irish Catholic return to scriptural study is radical in the proper sense of a return to roots.

What is truly unbelievable is that a liberated church should so turn its back on a wealth of tradition. What is difficult to understand is that this should happen in a country whose initial evangelisation was so complete, precisely because its early apostle(s) had accepted the existing pagan culture and Christianised it. By a curious turn of events it has been alleged that our own Irish missionaries into African and Eastern cultures had forgotten the Patrician model and tried to Europeanise their converts in order to Christianise them. Were they also conditioned by the recent history of the church at home? An annoying aspect of the change of direction is that it was undoubtedly undertaken with the very best of motives. The figure of Paul Cullen looms large in the story of the change of direction. Just when a strong leader could have undone the gradual decline of 1829-1850, Paul Cullen was sent to Ireland from Rome. Truly Roman in thinking, he set out to reorganise the Irish church on Roman lines as well as to correct some undoubted abuses. This he did mainly at the Synod of Thurles in 1850. With hindsight it is hard to credit some of the measures that were taken by that synod. In the new programme for reform house-stations were to be done away with! The entire *corpus* of traditional prayer was, for whatever reason, pushed aside and a plethora of continental-type devotions recommended to the faithful. Sodalities, novenas, processions, benedictions, medals, confraternaties and other such societies, were presented to a people for whom they were insipid compared to the salty Celtic flavour of the religious sustenance that they had known. It was a bad century for Irish spirituality, one from which we have not yet recovered. True, the many famines took a severe toll on the members of God's people in Ireland, but there was an invisible famine which was gradually starving the Irish soul of what was its life. Our Belderg was submerged! It was fortunate indeed for the West that McHale of Tuam did not succumb. He withstood the change at every stage: his own schools, his own catechism, his disregard for many of the Thurles decrees in practice. So, for instance, the house-stations have survived, predominantly in the West. And, of course, Vatican II has in many ways seen to it that 'the house is falling; the beaten men come into their own'.

This article has tried to steer clear, so far, of the importance in any spirituality of the language in which it is expressed; in this case the Irish language. It is impossible, of course, to leave language out of the entire equation. For as well as being a means of communication, a language is a repository and in that sense a key to the past. Because language is the normal outward expression of our thought it becomes, in a way, the body to the soul of our thinking. The Irish language then, is the chalice of one strain of Christian thought over a very long period of human existence; less indeed a chalice than a living calyx which has contained and shielded a flower and now shelters its seed. It is a strange aspect of the Irish literary revival that the movement paid minimal attention to the religious content of Irish. Hyde did collect *Amhráin Diaga Chúige Chonnacht* but in general the Gaelic League overlooked the religious riches of the language without which efforts at restoration were, in Ó Floinn's expressive phrase, 'as futile as the warming of a corpse'. And let it be said that the spiritual content of our native language does not consist merely, as is so often thought, of a list of greetings and blessings. In truth such lists are often over-sold, whereas in practice the once beautiful *Dia dhuit!* and its reply, or such as *le cúnamh Dé*, are in the spoken language so thoughtlessly used that they may well be on the way to such fossilisation as made the English 'Goodbye' from 'God be with ye'.

What, then, of the present and of the future? Firstly, and encouragingly, there are the survivals. There are people, as Sheehan said, 'scattered here and there through lonely hamlet and village, like some weather-beaten oaks that have survived a century of storm, to remind us, a puny race, of what our forefathers were.' There is the Gaeltacht – a sizeable area of it in Mayo – which is in authentic contact with the past through the spoken language, at least for some time still to come. And there are the glimpses one finds here and there even in our non-Gaeltacht homes and villages, just as the Reek might still peep up to give its witness when the avalanche has almost been complete. At a GAA national congress in Ballina at Easter in 1978 a Mass liturgy was, as usual, prepared by the local association for the Sunday morning. On the cover of the liturgy booklet was emblazoned: *Mac na hÓighe slán!* On that Easter morning, the effect of that authentic choice was truly uplifting. Somebody had remembered! Someone still knew the story of the cock in Irish tradition and knew that in that tradition, the Irish cock never crows 'Cockadoodledoo' but the proclamatory 'Mac na hÓighe slán' (The virgin's son is risen).

To my mind Knock Shrine is pivotal in the future of Irish spirituality; pivotal because of its extra-ordinary influence on so many ordinary Irish people who search for authenticity and truth; and pivotal because, as an internationally known shrine, it must be influenced by the character of shrines throughout the world. I feel no need to set down my own personal loyalty and commitment to the shrine of Knock, to its succeeding directors and their many workers. I shall trade now on that loyalty to mention what at times appears to me as a possible danger. Irish spirituality, for all that I have said, must not become a ghetto. Just as the Irish language has been enriched by the influx of Latin, Greek, Danish, Anglo-Norman and English; just as Carolan's music was energised by continental influences; just as our spirituality was enriched from the Irish colleges abroad, so also we can benefit by the influence of other strains of piety. But the proportion will be important. Is there a danger that some time in the future, Knock could go down the nineteenth century road? The pressure will be there, and all the more persuasive because almost unnoticeable. Is it a mere coincidence the the 'rounds' on the Reek are the traditional *deiseal* (right-handed, sun-wise) and that for some strange reason the 'rounds' of the Apparition chapel at Knock are *tuaifeal* (the other way round)? To be positive, since a deep study of Irish spirituality is not offered in any Irish seminary or university today, is it possible that Knock could become the epicentre of a movement for revival? A school and resource-centre for our traditional spirituality, just as it has been already been such a centre for Irish Marian devotion? Could Knock light its torch again from Brigid Trench's candle. (And it should be noted, I feel, that Brigid was the one witness who had to give her testimony in the Irish language!) Could there be a new Tochar Phádraic from the Reek to Knock? I firmly believe that there can and should. For there is always room for hope. And the real ground for such hope is: Tá Mac na hÓighe slán.

PART II
Exiles and Pilgrims

Exile and Return

Donal Dorr

About half of the people born in Mayo have first-hand experience of being exiles. Does this mean that Mayo is unable to support its people? Not at all. There are sufficient resources available to allow all of our people to live a full human life in our own county. Why then are so many compelled to emigrate, to become exiles? There are two simple reasons. Firstly, those who control the economic system under which we live, have given priority to other interests than those of ordinary Mayo people. Secondly, those who feel forced to leave, do so because they are unwilling to put up with what they experience as the unfulfilled and even degraded life of an unemployed person.

In writing this paper I am holding in the back of my mind this reality of the unwilling and unnecessary exile of half our people. Against this background, I propose to extend the notion of exile and explore it theologically. In all this I have a very practical aim in view – to contribute in some small way to changing the situation. I believe there is a need for a fundamental change in the economic structures which have turned Mayo into an unemployment blackspot. And there is just as much need for a change in the structures of the mind that prevent us from challenging and changing our society.

My aim is to attempt to do in the Irish situation what liberation theologians have been doing in Latin America and elsewhere. The primary concern of these theologians is not to write books which will be read by other theologians. It is rather to help the ordinary members of the Christian community to realise that God is on their side in their efforts to overcome injustice and to make society more humane. So they start their theology, not with church doctrines, or even with the bible, but with an analysis of the social situation in which their people are living. This analysis provides a solid basis for effective action by the community.

Following the lead of the liberation theologians, I propose in the first part of this paper to look at the economic, political, and cultural situation of the West of Ireland. What emerges is a depressing picture. I can only hope that my readers will not give up in despair before they come to the second part of the paper, in which I explore whether there is any realistic alternative to the present situation. This examination leads to the conclusion that an alternative is possible, but that in practice it is unlikely that it will be implemented. This leads on to the third part of the paper, in which I suggest that our Christian faith offers hope and inspiration for radical change.

PART ONE: ANALYSIS

'To hell or to Connaught' was Cromwell's policy for landowners from other parts of Ireland. In fact the choice was even more restricted than appears at first sight. For the result of Cromwell's plantation was to turn Connaught into a kind of hell. Many of those who owned land in the province were dispossessed, to make room for resettled landowners from other parts of the country. They did not emigrate but continued to eke out an existence on the sides of the hills. This was a key factor in bringing about the cycle of poverty so familiar to anybody who has lived in the third world. Over-population causes poverty; that is obvious. Less obvious but more significant is the fact that poverty causes over-population. Let me explain.

In the absence of industrial employment or investment resources, poor people are forced to provide for the next generation by dividing up whatever they have into ever smaller segments. That was done in Mayo up to the point where those who had a holding of land or a small business, such as a shop, could only barely survive. (In Foxford when I was growing up, almost everybody was poor, even those whom we thought of as 'well-off'; nobody had significant amounts of capital or property, except the nuns who owned the woollen mills, and that was run more as a charity than as a profit-making enterprise.) In a crowded province where good land was scarce, the division of property soon reached a limit; further sub-division would mean that the holdings or businesses would no longer be visible. At that point the only solution was to limit the population.

Perhaps the most obvious way to limit population is to reduce the birth-rate. But that is rarely a realistic option for poor people. They tend rather to have very large families. It is not so much that parents deliberately plan to have as many children as possible. But in a patriarchal society little account is taken of the burden placed on women by a long succession of pregnancies. The women are seen as passive in their sexuality; and the values of restraint and planning scarcely enter the consciousness of the men. So within a patriarchal culture of poverty, there is a general assumption that it is normal to have very large familites. This assumption is given ideological support by the official wisdom that large families are a blessing from God. At the practical level, poor people find some security in having plenty of close relatives. Furthermore, if poor parents have many children they can expect that several of them will survive into adulthood – and hope that some of these will do well and be in a position to help the rest of the family. For these different reasons, in the West of Ireland poverty led to over-population which in turn led to greater poverty.

In Mayo, emigration was the safety valve. It allowed a desperately poor people to continue to have large families. But the cost was the export of most of our young people and the taken-for-granted belief that Mayo could not support its own population. Not one of the members of my primary school class is now living in Mayo. Indeed, only four of us are still in Ireland. It is no coincidence that we are the four who managed to get second-level education. For at that time the bottleneck in education came at the end of primary school. The few of us who got through it were in a privileged position because we were so few. We had the possibility of breaking out of the cycle of poverty. That opportunity was never available to four fifths of the population of our parish. Their only choice was either to become exiles overseas or to live like exiles in their own land.

Cultural Exile

'To live like exiles in their own land'. At first sight this may seem to be just a rhetorical phrase. But in our situation there is a deep truth in it. For a very large number of those who continue to live in Mayo are not fully rooted or at home there. One aspect of this is a very well brought out in Brian Friel's play *Translations*. The play is set in the north-west of Ireland in the last century at the time of the 'ordnance survey' - when detailed maps of the area were being prepared under the auspices of the British army. Part of this process was the replacement of Irish place-names by anglicised equivalents. There is one marvellous scene where the English soldier Yolland reflects on the deeper meaning of the work in which he is engaged. He realises that the re-naming is going to have a very profound effect. His conclusion is that 'something is being eroded', and that what is taking place is 'an eviction of sorts'.[1]

What Friel seems to be suggesting is that those who stayed on in the West of Ireland became almost as much exiles as those who emigrated. It was not just those who emigrated who lost touch with their roots, with the tradition that had enabled their people to believe in themselves. The same applied to those who stayed on. They became, to some degree, exiles in their own land.

'An eviction of sorts'. One example springs to my mind. I grew up near the southern part of Lough Conn which contains an island that goes by the nonsensical name 'Glass Island'. That is the anglicised version of *Oileán na Glaise* – which, in Irish, means the island of the stream. Within my lifetime the island lost the last of its inhabitants. I think that, in addition to the economic pressures, the renaming of their home played some part in uprooting these people. It helped to erode their belief that life on the island was meaningful and worthwhile.

To make that island a home meant cultivating its land. To

know how to cultivate the soil and, even more important, to believe that it is worthwhile doing so, is a vital part of human culture. Losing the name of the island meant a partial loss of contact with the culture and tradition that gave a purpose and value to the labour of cultivation and the hardship of island life. It was much harder for the islanders to believe in their way of life – and in themselves – once the name of their island became meaningless. It was easier to give up, to allow the land to return to its wilderness state, and to seek a livelihood in the wilderness life of navvies and skivvies overseas.

Cultural Revival?
What about the great cultural changes that came about with the emergence of the Gaelic League and the founding of the Free State? Did they not bring about a revaluing of the traditional culture and the recovery of a belief in our own tradition and way of life? Yes and no. Yes, insofar as many Mayo people of today are men and women of initiative, vision, and courage; we do believe in ourselves; we are not ashamed of our accents, our music, our customs – or our airport. In all these respects there has been a real cultural renewal – and in the past twenty years or so this has come more from the grassroots than through government initiatives. But in another way this revitalisation has been ineffective. It has transformed the lives of many of our people as individuals; but it has not transformed the life of the people of Mayo as a whole. It has not enabled us to believe that all Mayo people have both the right and the possibility of living fully human lives in our own county, or even in our own country.

The problem arises at the point where culture overlaps with economics and politics. A people may undergo radical cultural changes and come out renewed and energised rather than dispirited and disempowered. For instance, the change of language and culture undertaken forty years ago by the Israeli nation seems, if anything, to have made the Israelis arrogant rather than broken-spirited. In the case of the West of Ireland, however, the renaming of places and the imposition of English by means of the new 'National Schools' was just one part of a much broader and longer process, a process that was political, economic, and cultural. It was one of the latest stages, perhaps the most effective one, of the attempt by the imperial power to dominate and assimilate its reluctant neighbour. It was just one part of a policy described accurately by the economist Raymond Crotty as 'imposed underdevelopment'.[2]

Since 1922, local community groups and successive Irish governments made serious efforts to counter the cultural oppression imposed by the British. These efforts have been partly successful:

they have restored our sense of self-respect. But there has been an almost total failure in the sphere where culture intersects with economics.

'Culture' has been defined too narrowly. The culture which has been renewed covers only part of the spectrum of life that was covered by the old culture. It has to do mainly with the activities that seem to be spiritual in the broad sense – music, dance, literature and celebration. In sharp contrast to this, the old culture included agriculture, horticulture, and aquaculture. It offered people ways of farming, gardening, fishing, house-building, and dressmaking that would enable them to live their lives and rear a family in their own villages. The deliberate efforts by governments and local groups to renew our traditional culture have not been directed towards these bread-and-butter aspects of our culture.

In fact, during the very years when the more spiritual aspects of our culture have been renewed, Ireland has adopted new conceptions of agriculture, horticulture, aquaculture, and industry-culture that are radically different from the traditional approaches. Radical newness is not necessarily wrong. And it is true that these new patterns of work provide good jobs for some individuals in the new agriculture and industry. But they are fundamentally inappropriate for Mayo as a whole. That is because they are quite unable to provide a fully human way of life for many, if not most, of the people of Mayo. They presuppose and impose a model of economic life that makes it impossible for all the people of Mayo to continue to live in their own county.

Why is the new model of economic life so inappropriate for our situation? Our key reason is that it replaces human labour with high-technology machinery. This means that it puts people out of work. We were promised many new jobs in high-tech industry and aquaculture. But, despite the enormous efforts and expenditure of the IDA, the number of long-term new jobs coming to Mayo has failed completely to live up to these promises; and there is no likelihood that this situation will improve significantly in the future.

There are two further reasons why the new model of economic activity is unsuitable as a basis for long-term human development. It leads us to use up a lot of non-renewable energy resources such as oil. And it puts undue pressure on the environment, e.g. pollution of our waters by 'dirty' industries and new types of agriculture.

False Dawn

For a short time in the early nineteen seventies these difficulties were overlooked and it seemed that the new model of economic development was the answer to the economic problems of Mayo. People began to believe that there was a livelihood for them in their own county. Emigration dropped off and many families returned to Mayo. It was a time of hope. The agricultural policies of the EEC were bringing many benefits to farmers. For the rest of us, the planners and politicians were bringing in Travenol, Babygro, Asahi and the other multinationals to provide what we were told would be good secure jobs. Free second-level schooling meant that young people who would have been looking for work were now staying on in school.

Meanwhile the rigidity of life and thought in rural Ireland was rapidly breaking down. The 'Late Late Show' had taken the lid off discussion of topics that had been taboo. Vatican II had begun to shake the Catholic community out of the spirituality, the devotionalism and the clericalism of the last century. At last, the two aspects of culture seemed to have come together: a way of life was emerging which offered a good living for all, and we could choose what we wished to retain from the riches of the culture of the past.

Now the bubble has burst. The hope for a new integrated culture and way of life has vanished over the past few years. We find ourselves more rootless than ever, with exile once again very much in our consciousness. It is true that the aspect of our culture which has to do with ideas and values has been opened up and transformed; in that process we may have gained more than we lost. But our biggest loss has been in the other aspect of culture – the part that has to do with economic matters, how our people make a living. We do not have a way of life which is open to all of our people. Most of the young have to emigrate; and this makes life very difficult even for those who stay at home.

The situation is rather different from what it was in the nineteen thirties, forties and fifties; in some respects it is better, but in others it is just as bad or worse. Nowadays, the main bottleneck for young people comes, not at the age of fourteen, but at the end of second-level schooling. And it is no longer possible to avoid the bottleneck by going on, as we did, to a higher level of education. For those who finish third level education find it equally impossible to get regular employment. Now, perhaps more than ever before, Mayo is providing a livelihood for only a small proportion of its young people.

Every young person in Mayo today is forced to see himself or herself as a potential exile. This is the harsh economic reality. It has given rise to a further problem which may be called 'the culture of emigration'. The level of emigration is so high that even those who have a relatively secure job do not live in a stable community, one where they can be sure of finding the social infra-structure that makes life worthwhile and enjoyable. The discos and the pubs seem to become lifeless when so much young blood is drained away. The football team may have to be disbanded because most of its members have emigrated. So the possibility of leaving to join their comrades overseas comes to be high in the consciousness even of those who have got jobs. This conjunction of economic and cultural uncertainty is what I have in mind when I speak of Mayo people 'living like emigrants in their own land'.

Whose Responsibility?
The adoption of the modern pattern of so-called development was, of course, actively encouraged and even imposed by recent Irish governments. The effect of government policies has been to continue and even accelerate the policies of the former imperial power. Now, within the European Community, Ireland is becoming, perhaps more than ever before, an outlying province with little control over the economic welfare of its people. But it is all too easy simply to blame the government. The fact is that the myth of 'development' was swallowed not only by the politicians but by the voters as well. They have allowed this myth of development to disguise the reality of policies which amounted to the very opposite of genuine human development for all. [3]

In saying that the voters have swallowed the myth of the development, I have chosen my words carefully; I do not say that all our citizens have made this mistake. We have very many citizens who are no longer voters – they are those who have been deprived of the right to vote by being forced to emigrate. These non-voting exiled citizens are the most obvious casualties of the modern model of so-called development. But, unlike other members of the European Community, Ireland makes no provision for our emigrants to vote. Depriving them of the power to vote against the system greatly reduces the pressure to change it. Winners take all. It is as though we were playing a game of musical chairs, where one by one people lose their place in the privileged circle. Those who remain are kept busy looking after their own interests. They have little or no effective solidarity with those who have lost their places. They do not realise that it might be in the interests of almost all of them to change the basic rules of the game.

So long as we continue to accept and impose the modern style of 'development', we make it impossible for the bulk of our young people to live a worthwhile purposeful life in their own county, or even their own country. The recent election campaign shows clearly that the great majority of both the politicans and the voters are not seriously committed at present to changing the situation. Indeed it seems that most Irish people cannot even envisage any realistic alternative.

This is not so surprising, for the climate of ideas in which we live makes the present situation seem inevitable and unchangeable.

It is almost impossible for us to realise that the plight in which we find ourselves has come about as a result of a series of free choices. There was the choice of Cromwell which created poverty on a large scale. There were choices made by the British authorities in the last century to support industrial development in the 'mainland' while using Ireland as a resource for cheap food and cheap labour. Then there were key choices made by our own governments – the most significant of which was the replacement of the 'Sinn Féin' economic policies of the nineteen thirties and forties by the Whitaker policy of an open economy and 'development' through the encouragement of investment by transnational corporations. The major political parties chose to support our entry into the EEC, and the great majority of the voters agreed. In recent elections none of the major parties proposed a serious alternative to the model of economic development that we have been using for over twenty-five years.

PART TWO: A REALISTIC ALTERNATIVE?

But is there any realistic alternative to the model of development which we have been using? To answer this question I want to reformulate it as two distinct questions:

Firstly, is there an alternative model of devlopment which would provide a fulfilled and human life for all of our people who wish to stay at home? I believe that the answer to this question is, yes.

Secondly, is it likely that the people of Ireland would be willing at present to adopt such a model? I fear that the answer to this second question is, no.

Let me spell out more fully the answers to the above two questions. The answer to the first question is that there really is enough to go round, provided we are not too greedy. The gross national product of Ireland today is very much larger, in real terms, than it was thirty years ago. If it were shared in a fairly equitable way it would be more than sufficient to give a comfortable standard of living to all of our people, including those of our exiles who would wish to come home.

But it is at present highly unlikely that the decision-makers of Ireland will settle for such an equitable share-out of our resources. For such a distribution would leave people 'comfortable' only by the standards of about thirty years ago. There is not enough available to give everybody the comforts they now demand. In other words, the central reason why there is not enough for all of our people is that, over the past generation, our expectations have risen very much faster than our ability to meet them.

The wide gap between expectations and what is realistically possible is not just due to greed; people are probably no more greedy now than they have ever been. The problem is that the rise in expectations has been stimulated quite deliberately by the model of economic development that we have chosen. At the heart of this conception of development lies the notion of ever-increasing 'growth' based on ever-increasing spending power by those individuals who have income to dispose of. The policies chosen by our leaders, and accepted by the voters, have been ones that led those who earn money (through wages or profits) to insist on being able to spend more and more. Political leaders and voters simply turned a blind eye to the fact that the practical effect of this was that most of the available resources would go to fewer people; the unlucky ones were left to choose between emigration or survival on inadequate social security.

Instead of asking our people to face up realistically to the gap between expectations and achievements, the planners and politicians found three ways of dodging the issue, postponing the problem until it had grown much more serious:

Firstly, they caused the State to indulge in borrowing on an enormous scale; to justify this they maintained that the growth of the economy would make it easy for us to pay off the debts in the future. This left people with the illusion that our expectations were not unduly high. It also left us burdened by a massive debt which makes our present problem far worse than it would otherwise have been.

Secondly, successive governments adopted policies which involved a rapid 'cashing in' of ecological assets (clean air, fresh water, mineral resources) which we had possessed for generations. This means that we used up, for short-term gain, many of these resources which were our reserves. Now we have polluted streams and rivers as the half-hidden price paid for increased incomes from intensive farming; and the used-up deposits at Tynagh and Tara are the price we paid for the short-term prosperity of miners. There is a severe limit to the extent to which this 'solution' is viable. Ordinary people are coming to realise this, as we can see from the resistance building up in Mayo against ecologically reckless gold-mining and fish-farming.

Thirdly, in response to the demand for higher profits and wages, the planners and politicians uncritically adopted a policy of automation. This allowed the powerful and vocal groups who had capital or secure jobs to get large increases in their income. But the price paid for this policy was that many more people were put out of work. So a privileged group benefited while many others were forced to emigrate or to take a major drop in income by going on the dole.

In recent years hardly anybody has pointed out that unemployment and emigration are not the result of circumstances beyond our control. Politicians and economists have colluded in giving the impression that in this respect we are helpless victims of the world economic system. But the truth is that if we scaled down our expectations and adjusted our economic and welfare policies, we would have enough to go round.

Work-Sharing

When I say 'enough to go round' I am not referring just to money. Simply giving a hand-out of money is unsatisfactory for a variety of reasons, of which the main one is that meaningful work is a necessary (but not sufficient) condition for human fulfilment. What is required is work-sharing of various kinds.

In fact many Mayo people have practised different kinds of work-sharing over the years. We have part-time building-workers and factory workers who supplement their income by working their very small family farms. We still have some part-time dressmakers, part-time painters, part-time cooks, and so on. But the present model of economic development, and the model of social welfare that is linked to it, treats such part-time workers as marginal and puts them at a disadvantage in various ways. What is needed is a fairly thorough shift of emphasis and priorities which would offer incentives for particular kinds of work-sharing — the kinds that would allow many more people to find a comfortable livelihood in Ireland. Workers in certain companies have in recent times been realistic enough to agree to take cuts in their wages and benefits in order to save their jobs. The work-sharing proposal I am making is rather like an extension of this approach to the work-force as a whole. The available work-hours would be shared out between more workers. This implies that those who have jobs at present would give up over-time and even part of their regular work-hours (perhaps one or two days a week). The good side of this is that it would provide them with time for creative spare-time work, e.g. part-time farming or improvements to the home or the development of community facilities. And there would be less job insecurity, since there would be more jobs all round. But the difficult part is that in the short-term it would mean that the standard of living for many workers would no longer be as high as it used to be.

I am not suggesting that work-sharing is a magic formula that will provide jobs for everybody. The truth is that economics is such an inexact science that nobody can really come up with an effective way to guarantee full employment; and some attempts to 'make' jobs can create worse problems in the long run. But work-sharing offers notable short-term and long-term advantages. In the short-term it can help us break out of the disastrous economic and psychological problems that arise when up to half of the workforce cannot find work. And, by bridging the gap between overburdened workers and alienated unemployed, it can help to create a climate where all the members of the community can together take responsibility for the welfare of all. I must add, however, that if work-sharing is to be effective it will have to be combined with radical changes in life-style, along the lines which I shall indicate in the next section of this paper.

In order to ensure that people should have a fair amount of work and comfort over a long period of time, it would also be essential to promote a much more ecologically sensitive type of development. If we treat our environment only as a resource to be exploited, we are likely before long to kill the goose that lays the golden eggs. We have to learn to live more effectively in partnership with nature, respecting it and caring for it, so that we can have authentic development.

A major objection to any proposal of changes of this kind is that they could only be carried out if Ireland were to retreat into isolation, cutting itself off from the rest of the world, and particularly from the other members of the European Community. But this is not true. In fact people committed to such changes would at present find more allies outside Ireland than within it. At least some of the increasing number of people who support Green Parties in Europe and elsewhere would find themselves in sympathy with these kinds of changes.

Alternatives in Life-Style

Change in economic and social welfare policies would not be sufficient. We would have to become less wasteful and somewhat more puritan in our mode of living. Cheap and efficient semi-public transport could take over from much of the private motoring. Walking and cycling could make a come-back. Clothes would be designed to last longer and we would have less of the 'throw-away' culture. Consumption of sweets and soft drinks would be greatly reduced. With less money to spend on luxuries, people would have to change their preferred patterns of recreation. Social activities in the local hall might largely replace the pub culture that young people in Ireland adopt so easily.

Of course, this seems unrealistic. Yet the extraordinary thing is that young people commonly are quite content to make just these kinds of changes when they get married and begin to rear a family. And those of us who have kept in contact with what is happening in Mayo, will know many individuals and families who have given up good jobs abroad to return here to a much less luxurious life, simply in order to benefit from the values that cannot be bought – the sense of being part of a community, the beauty of nature, the peace that comes from living close to the earth. Furthermore, those of us who have lived in the Third World have seen for ourselves that people can live a very fulfilled life with only a fraction of the amenities which we have come to take for granted. Indeed, the older generation will recall that we ourselves survived quite well during World War II when most of the luxuries were missing. Finally, it seems likely that, when the ecological crisis really begins to bite in some years time, all of us will find that we have to put up with much greater restrictions. All this indicates that changes of the kind I am suggesting are by no means objectively unrealistic. It is just that it seems politically unrealistic to expect people to undertake them voluntarily at this time.

Proposals about large-scale worksharing of the kind I outlined in the previous section are not at present taken very seriously by the 'social partners' who have taken on the task of dividing up the national cake. It is considered to be 'unrealistic' to ask workers as a whole to make such sacrifices. So these ideas don't even get on the agenda of the negotiations between the social partners. Maybe one reason for this is that the employers, the trade unions and the government do not make place at the negotiating table for the two other social partners, the long-term unemployed and the emigrants. Another reason is that workers have very good reason to suspect that they are the ones who are being asked to make the sacrifices, while the investors and the banks continue to increase their profits.

But, whatever the reason, the fact is that a change of policy and approach which is quite realistic in principle, is in practice a non-starter. We remain paralysed through a lack of trust, a lack of vision, of concern for our own people, an absence of the kind of imaginative planning that would be needed to work out a credible alternative. Above all we are blocked through a lack of true leadership. The option of a real alternative is not put clearly before the people. We do not have leaders who are prepared to take the risk of going against the current, of helping people to see how much they have to gain by changing our model of development so that it becomes a fair and balanced development for all instead of an unbalanced, unjust, and ecologically exploitative development that favours some at the expense of many others.

PART THREE: RETURN FROM EXILE?

Readers who have persevered this far with me, may well be wondering when am I going to bring theology into this paper. Actually, I believe I have been doing theology from the beginning, and I hope this will now become evident. I have been describing the human situation in which we find ourselves; a situation of being 'exiles' either at home or abroad. In some respects it is highly unusual; but in another way it is typical of the human situation. We find ourselves locked into a position that we don't have to be in. In principle, or in theory, there is a way out. Yet, realistically, we know it won't happen.

The liberation theologians of Latin America try to look realistically at the situation of oppression in which their people find themselves, and they find little basis for hope. But where human hope falls they turn to the bible and find, in the story of Moses and his people, a hope that lies beyond human expectation.

The person who wishes to do theology in relation to Mayo can use fully look for some parallels in the bible. I suggest that we can find some light by looking first at two obvious parallels, and then beyond them at the central core of the Christian faith. First of all, there is the story of the Exile of the People of God. In the bible, 'the exile' does not refer to the time spent by the Jews in Egypt. The exile came much later. It followed the destruction of the political power, first of the northern kingdom and then of the southern kingdom of the Jews. With the capture of Jerusalem the Temple was destroyed, and all the surviving leaders of the people were carried off into exile by the victorious imperial power.

I have been describing the exile experience of the people of Mayo, so it is worthwhile seeing whether the biblical account of the exile throws any light on our situation. In fact, I think it is particularly helpful to look not so much at the exile itself, as at the experience of the return from exile.

The Jewish exile lasted for seventy years. Then, when all human hope should have died, there came the return. Not an earth-shaking event but just a minor emigration of a determined few (Ezra 8). The return of this remnant did not come in military glory; it was rather the result of patronage and patient diplomacy (Neh 2:3-6). The returned exiles struggled to revive their culture, encapsulated in their Law (Neh 8:1–10:38); and with great determination they set about rebuilding their city and their Temple (Neh 3:1–4:23). They were no saints; even then the strong took advantage of the weak (Neh 5:1–6).

Despite all its inadequacies, this return was a rebirth for God's people, a new beginning. World history has been radically changed because of this apparently minor event. For the people themselves, the history of that time became a vivid reminder that God can draw new life out of utter failure. There is hope even for a people that, by human reckoning, have lost all hope. Two thousand five hundred years ago it seemed that Jewish history had effectively come to an end. But out of the exile they came back – politically weak, economically impoverished, but enriched in spirit. They had been forged into a people who were able to endure and survive and cling onto their own traditions. They were now a people who had learned much from the religion and the gods of their neighbours – but they had a renewed determination to be faithful to the God who was faithful to them when all human hope had failed. They had become a people who were able to endure centuries and millennia of persecution, and could still look forward to a future as a free people in their own land. Their history gives me hope that the people of Mayo may also return from exile – hope that we too, by God's grace and our own efforts, may live in freedom and dignity in our own land.

The bible also contains another exile story. It is the more personal tale of the Prodigal Son, the young man who squandered his wealth and only came to his senses when he found himself helpless and hopeless in exile. The exile situation of the people of Ireland, and even of Mayo, has some elements in common with his experience. Like him, we have squandered what we inherited and can be held in some way responsible for our situation of exile. Like him we have the possibility of coming to our senses and coming back home with the intention of living a more frugal life in future. And like him we may find that, having learned our lesson, we will be more welcome and comfortable at home than we might have expected. The story reminds us that our return from our exile situation cannot be just a purely political and economic happening. It will have to involve an element of personal conversion: sorrow for the wasteful luxury of the past, a willingness to change our ways, a determination to live frugally in future – and an openness to accept the surprising and unmerited generosity of our home.

A Source for Hope?

These exile stories are inspiring; but, to tell the truth, they are not quite enough for me. They are not sufficient to break the hopelessness and sense of paralysis that seems a central part of our exile experience. I need some stronger evidence to convince me that a return is possible. For me, a return from exile would begin from a firm belief that the lost opportunities are not gone for ever, a solid conviction that the long slow exile of the people of Mayo can be transformed into something far richer and better than we have lost. By some miracle I must be able to experience the loss as a gain. The only way I can hope for such a miracle is by exploring the mystery of the Cross.

At the heart of the Christian faith lies the cross. It recalls for us a historical event – the execution of Jesus. It represents a doctrine of our faith, an article of the creed. But it has become something more: it is the fundamental symbol which bridges the gap between faith and the tragedies of daily life. Everyday people die holding a crucifix, people face up to impossible situations strengthened by prayer before the crucifix, and people who have suffered apparently irreparable hurt and loss are able to be reconciled by experiencing solidarity with Christ on the cross.

Literally, the cross is an instrument of torture and death, a gallows or gibbet which has just one purpose – to bring a criminal to a slow, painful, and shameful death deprived of all dignity. Yet when you or I take up a crucifix we do not feel a thrill of horror and fear, as we would if somebody gave us, say, a picture of a person tortured in South Africa. On the cross we see an image of a tortured man, but we don't regret his torture and death. We can even be glad that this awful thing has happened. The power of Christ's death is such that it has transformed the cross from being an image of shame to an image or nobility and glory. It evokes in us not horror and grief but gratitude and love. And yet the suffering and shame are not absent. They remain fully real, historical facts that are not denied or played down by the symbol of the cross. But they have become suffused with love and joy.

The cross represents the rejection of Christ, the failure of his mission. Yet our faith now reveals to us, as it did to the disciples at Emmaus, that for Jesus 'it was necessary to suffer these things' (Lk 24:26). By faith we learn to set this failure in a wider context – 'beginning with the books of Moses and the writings of all the prophets' (Lk 24:27) and culminating in the resurrection of Jesus to new life and his sharing of that life with all who believe in him. In that full context we can now experience Christ's death as part of a pattern; we see it as central to God's loving plan. The shameful death of Jesus is meaningful and even infinitely worthwhile when seen as the focal point in the providential history of God's people.

My faith in the cross of Jesus is something that throws light on every aspect of my life. It cannot be confined to some narrowly defined 'religious' sphere, or to the private aspects of my life. It permeates my political beliefs, enabling me to believe that a situation that seems hopeless can be transformed. Just as the death of Jesus was not the end but the beginning of a new life, so there can be a return for the people of Mayo from our exile experience.

It was hard for the exiles to walk back from Babylon and begin a new life in their own land. It was hard for their leader to persuade the powers of the time to allow them to undertake this project of restoration. But the hardest thing of all was for them to believe that it was possible. It is hard, too, for me to believe that the received wisdom of the economists and the politicians is not the final word on Mayo.

The change from 'exile' to 'return' in the Mayo situation is politically so unlikely that it calls for an evident exercise of God's power. In other words, it requires a kind of miracle. But this is one of those miracles that God cannot do alone, since it requires people as instruments of God's power. It is never easy to believe in a miracle; and it is particularly difficult when we ourselves are called to be the instruments that bring it about. The miracle of return from exile of the Jewish people could only begin when a small believing remnant was prepared to put their faith into practice. Once they started, the miracle had already begun to take place.

Can such miracles take place in today's world? There are indications that they can. I think of what the Chinese did a generation ago, and what the Nicaraguans achieved in their struggle for genuine development before they were swamped by the Contras. And at present I think especially of what the Palestinian people are doing in their struggle to overcome oppression. They have come to realise that the economic and culture aspects of the struggle for liberation are at least as important as the military and political aspects. The Palestinians are now making heroic sacrifices in an effort to develop some measure of economic self-sufficiency. In doing so they show that a people who are determined to take charge of their own destiny can do so, in spite of all the odds. The transformation of the consciousness of the Palestinian people is so radical that it has been compared to the change that took place in the first Christians on the day of Pentecost. And this change of a whole nation has been evoked and coordinated by a corps of dedicated leaders and animators. They were the ones who believed that the miracle was possible; and by their faith they made it possible for others.

It will have to be like this in Mayo. Some few have to believe that a 'return from exile' is possible. And then they have to begin to find ways in which that possibility can be brought into being. In the meantime we can pray for this miracle, and that some of us will be called to play a part in bringing it about:

> Remember your people, whom you chose long ago,
> When you brought us out of slavery to be your own people...
> All our sacred symbols are gone; there are no prophets left
> and nobody knows how long this will last.
> But you, God, have been our ruler from the beginning,
> you have saved us many a time ...
> Remember the covenant you made with us...
> Rouse yourself, God, and defend your cause. (Ps 74)

Notes
1. Brian Friel, *Translations*, London (Faber & Faber:1981), 43.
2. Raymond Crotty, *Ireland In Crisis: A Study in Capitalist Colonial Undevelopment*, Dingle (Brandon:1986), 17.
3. cf Crotty, *Ireland in Crisis*, 100.

Faith: A Pilgrim Condition

Mary Guy

The continuing call of faith is a call to allow God's relationship with us to become the central concern of our lives. When we allow this to happen we are saying an unqualified 'yes' to God's decision to reach out and communicate personally with all of humanity and specifically with ourselves. Faith therefore, is not something we create, but something awakened in us because of the reality of who God is. While the initiative for self-disclosure comes from God, this self-disclosure remains unfinished unless it is reciprocated. The purpose of self-communication is reciprocity. Faith therefore is our response to God's self-revelation.

God's decision to reach out to the human always was, and still is, a decision to enter into personal relationship with people. As God is salvation, he is the power to receive salvation. He not only opens people to his revelation but also gives them the capacity to receive it and to respond. Relationships grow and develop when people are attracted to each other. This is true, not only in relationships between two people but also in relationships between people and their God. Mutual attraction is not sufficient to sustain relationships however, unless this attraction is underpinned by the knowledge that comes only through self-disclosure. Knowledge about a person we are attracted to will never be enough. We can know many facts about other people, but it is only the people themselves who can tell us who they really are, and how they feel about us. Nobody can be forced into self-disclosure however. It is a decision made out of love and the desire to be known by the persons loved. It is God's decision for us! This decision on the part of God demands a certain self-transcendence for people of faith, because self-revelation demands reverent listeners. This level of listening is impossible for those who are totally engrossed in themselves and in their own concerns. Furthermore, because self-revelation is always incomplete without a response, listening to God as he reveals himself also involves a sharing of the reactions evoked within us as a result of listening. In sharing these reactions we are sharing ourselves. Self-disclosure on the part of God therefore results in self-disclosure on the part of those who listen to God. It results in relationship. But why share ourselves when we are already known by God? The purpose of our self-disclosure is not to rectify any lacunae in God's knowledge of us. Such sharing is basic to all relationships that move towards intimacy. As God can never be fully known, our commitment to relationship with him must be continuing and developing. It is a life commitment involving all other life commitments. Within the Christian context it finds expression in 'Jesus is Lord.'

Faith and Self-Awareness
Because the continuing call of faith is a call to conscious relationship with a personal God, there is a need to bring to consciousness who this God is. We became the people we are through encounter with others, and achieve the fullness of our humanity through encounter with God. And yet the full reality of significant others in our lives, including God, often remains in the cloudy realm of half-awareness. Lack of awareness allows us, to a greater or less extent, to remain happy within our own enclosed self, seeing everything else in terms of usefulness to us. On the other hand, the more aware we are of God and of the people of God – those who have affirmed us, challenged us, healed us, confronted us and loved us – the more we are pulled out of our self-centredness. Conscious relationship with God involves nothing short of conversion.

Assumptions and Questions
Sometimes our very familiarity with God can be the greatest obstacle to questioning who he is for us and why we should believe. Familiarity can lead to unquestioned assumptions about the other. We cannot avoid making assumptions. We make thousands of them every day. Every time we see a green pedestrian light we assume that motorists and cyclists will stop and that it is safe to cross the road. However there is a need to keep assumptions and facts separated in our minds and continually to test the assumptions for validity and reliability. The probability of unquestioned assumptions is more likely in a country such as Ireland where God and the things of God have permeated every aspect of the culture and history for centuries. Belief was the recognised norm for the vast majority of Irish people and, where there is such a climate of belief, there is little need to question who God is for us and why we should believe in him. But this climate of unquestioned belief has changed during the last twenty years and the indications are that it will continue to change.

To inquire into my act of faith, by asking who is the God I believe in and why I should believe, is not a new idea. Such questioning occurs in both the Old and New Testaments. For example, in Isaiah (40:25) Yahweh asks the people, 'to whom will you compare me?' while in the New Testament (Mk 8:29; Mt 16:16; Lk 9:20) Jesus puts a similar question to his disciples when he asks, 'who do you say that I am?' The starting point of all theology is the existence of a community that claims to be the people of God. There is no neutral starting point for any of us. As cradle Christians we started life within a particular faith community which has its origins in both the Old and New Testaments.

The first Christians existed at a specific time in history and understood themselves as a community of the Living Presence, with a responsibility for handing on what they had received from Jesus Christ. History is a process in which we are all involved. Our history and culture colour the way we look at all reality, including the reality we call God. Attention to our past throws new light on our present stance as historical people of faith who have a responsibility to future generations. All Christians, from every generation, are responsible for handing on what they have learned from their faith in Jesus Christ. Christianity always looks to its origins as constitutive of its own self-understanding. Salvation history however is the working out of God's presence, not only in the Israel of long ago, but in the history of all humanity, including the present generation. Basic faith questions regarding the God in whom we believe are not asked only of a people in the past. They are our questions also. To avoid them is to avoid responsibility for our role within history.

Faith in History

Because the Old Testament concept of revelation includes that of a word spoken and heard, Yahweh's question, 'to whom will you compare me?' was addressed to a people who were very familiar with the need to listen to their God. The Old Testament sees God in a very intimate relationship with the people of Israel. He is their God who communicates with them and acts on their behalf and they in turn relate to him as a person and trust him, secure in the certainty that their faith is grounded on a solid foundation. God is their rock. The word of God in the Old Testament not only tells something about the Speaker, but it brings about the reality which it signifies. The concept of revelation in the Old Testament therefore is related to history. The whole understanding of Israel, that God met her at different historical moments, is a valid expression of this. The implication of this for the Israelites was that their human situation was taken seriously by their God, e.g. the Exodus. For the people of the Old Testament there was no history apart from God. God's action in Old Testament history is always characterised by a promise, which leads to further expectation on the part of the people. Israel has a concept of revelation therefore that is eschatological. God is known and yet unknown. The presence of the divine implies continuous restlessness, persistent search. People can never have enough of God's presence. (Jer 29:13; Amos 8:11; Ps 42: 2-4; Ps 63) This is why the Old Testament sees Israel's constant temptation as the desire to substitute laws and idols for this God who must always be sought.

Israel's Pilgrim Search for God

The context of a question affects the dialogue evoked by the question. If I enquire how a mother is feeling after the safe birth of a long-awaited child, the dialogue between us will be different from the one that occurs when the same question is put to another mother who has just given birth to a stillborn baby. When Yahweh asks the question, 'To whom will you compare me?' he is asking people in slavery who are feeling rejected and ignored by their God. Interestingly enough the answer comes, not through preoccupation with the suffering they are enduring, but through looking outside themselves, even to the stars:

> To whom could you liken me and who could be my equal? says the Holy One. Lift up your eyes and look. Who made these stars if not he who drills them like an army, calling each one by name? So mighty is his power, so great his strength that not one fails to answer. How can you say, Jacob, how can you insist, Israel, 'My destiny is hidden from Yahweh, my rights are ignored by my God?' Did you not know? Have you not heard? Yahweh is an everlasting God, he created the boundaries of the earth. He does not grow tired or weary, his understanding is beyond fathoming. He gives strength to the wearied, he strengthens the powerless. Young people may grow tired and weary, youths may stumble, but those who hope in Yahweh renew their strength, they put on, grow weary, walk and never tire.

The type of looking required by Yahweh is not a casual glance, but a detailed study involving total concentration. On a starry night it would take a lot of looking to ascertain whether or not all the stars that should be present are actually there. This type of looking is impossible for a person who is self-absorbed. While such a concentration is not easy at the best of times, it is even more difficult for people who are suffering and feeling abandoned. Although they have made their feelings known, Yahweh still asks them to trust his promise and to believe that this trust is indeed well-founded despite their present suffering. They cannot control God but they can remember his involvement in their history as they share their feelings of rejection with him. The temptation is to reject their historical experience of a personal God and to allow their present suffering to deflect them from the continuing search for him. This search cannot be confined to the good times only. At painful moments in Israel's history that search involved a willingness to let go of their own interpretation of Yahweh's attitude towards them. They were challenged not to give up but to listen to Yawheh as he led them to a deeper level of trust by changing their current image of him, of themselves and of reality.

Disciples of Jesus: Pilgrims in Faith

Although the words and context are different, there is a continuity in the meaning of faith between the Old Testament and the New. In the New Testament God's self-revelation is concretised in Jesus Christ. (Rom 3:21; Heb 2:21; Jn 1:18) Although the recognition and content of faith can vary in different books of the New Testament (faith for John approaches knowledge; for Paul it is the ground of things hoped for; in the Synoptics it is in the one who brings about the Kingdom of God) the constant element in both Old Testament and New Testament faith is that God's self-revelation be listened to, trusted and responded to with total commitment. What changes in the New Testament is that faith now involves a relationship with the person of Jesus Christ. He is God's word. There is and can be no greater revelation than Jesus because there is no greater unity possible between the human and the divine than in the person of Jesus. As human he is both recipient and participant in revelation and not just revelation. He presents himself as one who lives in prayerful communion with his Father and invites others to join him in this relationship. Although our faith is not constitutive of Jesus' revelation, yet his revelation is not complete without our faith, because our confession of faith is the reception of the other half of his name ... Christ.

When God revealed himself in Jesus, history was affected. By his words and actions, the human Jesus called into being the Christian community where we are involved with him in a response. For the early Christian community faith was not a mental assent to ideas and propositions proposed by Jesus. It was a 'yes' to the invitation issued by Jesus to enter a relationship of constant companionship with him. This pilgrim relationship with Christ gradually gave a new meaning to their lives as it helped them to perceive reality and interpret their experiences in the light of that relationship.

When Jesus asks the question, 'Who do you say that I am?' he asks it of those who were already familiar with his words and deeds – though they frequently misunderstood them. Like the blind man in the preceding section of Mark, their eyes are being opened by degrees. In asking this question Jesus is asking the disciples to look beyond his words and deeds to himself. This is never an easy question to ask or a comfortable one to answer. And yet, in relationships that matter, it is important to know that the other sees us as we really are, as distinct from what we say or do. An honest response to this question is difficult because our perception of others is always influenced by previous information regarding them. It is not surprising therefore that this question of Jesus, 'who do you say that I am?' is preceded by the question,: 'Who do people say I am?' We all form images of God as a result of the information we have received about him. The more aware we become of these images, the greater our ability to assess them in the light of our own experience of God and our growing knowledge of the source of Christianity. For example, if the image of God I received in childhood is a God who loves me only when I am 'good', is this my actual experience of God? Is this the same God who, in Christ, not only associated with the despised people in society but proved his love by dying for us while we were still sinners? (Rom 5:8.) During his lifetime, and today, Jesus is not satisfied with the image of him that comes from others. He needs to know how his disciples see him, in the light of their own experience of him. An honest response to such a question always involves responsibility. For example, if I identify another as friend he/she has the right to expect true friendship. When Peter acknowledges Jesus as Messiah, therefore, he must allow Jesus to be just that – Messiah for Peter. The responsibility that goes with articulating who Christ is for us, is highlighted in the text following Peter's profession of Faith – the first prediction by Jesus of his passion and death. (Mk 8:31-33) Peter argues with Christ, but is told in no uncertain terms that Christ intends to fulfil his role as Messiah in his own way. Peter must take responsibility for acknowledging Jesus as Messiah by following and not trying to control. As the values and attitudes that motivated the life and death of Jesus became more and more their own values and attitudes, the disciples of Jesus were inspired to continue his action in a creative way amid new and different historical circumstances.

Conversion

In both the Old Testament and New Testament, encounter with God resulted in a healing and transforming effect which makes an impact on the individual and the community. Relationship with Jesus also requires conversion. Conversion is the willingness to accept the presence of the divine in our lives. We have no choice regarding God's initiative to love us, but we do have a choice about how we will respond to this initiative and allow it to transform us. The more we open ourselves to God's love for us, the more this love will transform all aspects of our lives. Having God as a lover carries with it the responsibility of loving him and all that he loves. This includes ourselves, our environment, our world and all the people who inhabit it. Through faith therefore we transcend ourselves not only in our relationship with God but also in our relationships with all of God's creation. Like Jesus, our continuing call of faith must result in concrete expressions of love, that focus in a special way on our brothers and sisters who remain unloved at this moment in history. The concept of love as a source of power runs counter to much of what is happening in the world and in Ireland today. We only have to look at the conditions at home and abroad to see the effects of loveless relationships and policies!

Our conversion in love and to love is a faith-conversion to God and neighbour, person and community.

In conclusion, the mystical number 7 may be invoked to summarise the lessons to be drawn for pilgrim believers from some of these Old and New Testament questions which have shaped our history.

1) The initiative for relationship between the human and divine comes from God and not from us. The fullness of God's revelation come in Jesus Christ. God continues to reveal himself in history and faith is our response to God's revelation.

2) Responding to God's self-revelation requires a listening that is incompatible with total self-absorption. Faith demands a certain self-transcendence even in the midst of suffering.

3) Because faith is conscious relationship with God, there is a need for awareness regarding this God with whom we are relating. The images of God we have received from others need to be identified and assessed in the light of the sources of Christianity and our own experience.

4) Faith is continuing, a pilgrim faith. There is always more to be known about God. We all have our own idols: work, books, places, laws etc., but for people of faith these cannot be allowed to replace God or the search for God.

5) All our feelings are acceptable to God: love, rejection, anger, fear, or whatever. But we cannot control God.

6) Faith can never be either totally subjective or totally objective because it involves more than personal feelings or unquestioned acceptance of dogmas.

7) Faith is a committment to relationship with God that involves all other life commitments.

All this may seem far removed from Mayo. Yet it was in that faith-context that this pilgrimage began for the contributors to our book. The pilgrimage of faith is determined, as much by its starting-point as by its final destiny in God.

God in Ordinarie
Brendan Hoban

Theology should be accessible to 'ordinary people'. The *raison d'être* of this enterprise is to situate faith in the context of a particular lived experience – a Mayo experience – in the hope that this 'faith', in this life, in this place, will speak to other 'faiths' in other lives in other places. There is a sense in which the particular speaks to the universal, what is most personal is also most general. As well as that, I am reminded that Mother Teresa's congregation, who serve in the most oppressive byways of God's vineyard, are enjoined to keep the windows of their oratories open in order to maintain the connection between life and prayer. And there is too the now almost clichéd extract from an Evelyn Waugh novel, in which he has the empress Helena praying to the Magi:

> How laboriously you came, taking sights and
> calculating where the shepherds had run barefoot ...
> For his sake who did not reject your curious gifts.
> Pray always for all the learned, the oblique, the
> delicate. Let them not be forgotten at the throne of
> God when the simple come into their Kingdom.

This is not in any sense to jeer at academic theology, that often abstruse but necessary discipline that facilitates the wider view, the larger perspective. But when theology fails to echo the lived experiences of what we patronisingly call 'ordinary people', it is simply ignored. Theologians are then operating within a closed circuit – writing merely for one another:

> So much ... theological discussion has suddenly become
> meaningless because people could not relate it to
> their experience of being human. [1]

Indeed the *cri de coeur* of the private Gar to the insensitive Canon in Brian Friel's *Philadelphia, Here I Come*:

> You could translate all this loneliness, all this groping, this dreadful bloody buffoonery into Christian terms that will make life bearable to us all. Why arid, Canon? Isn't this your job, to translate? Why don't you speak then?

echoes the length and breadth of Mayo and beyond.

I accept that 'translation' can be overdone, that rendering things wholly intelligible can divest them of meaning, that in Kavanagh's phrase, 'Through a chink too wide there comes in no wonder'. It is possible in effect to undo the symbol, to milk it of substance and meaning by indiscriminate explication. At the same time there is a common verbal and experiential currency – the raw material of theology – that has to be dealt with, not obscured or ignored.

There is a sense in which theological truths have to be vulgarised – which is not to imply a necessarily inexact reductionism. The vulgate after all is merely the bible in the common tongue. The Catholic church, as the critic Clive James once pointed out, has always felt obliged to remind intellectual converts that their objections to plastercut statues of Christ with a battery-operated Sacred Heart that lights up in the darkness are objections to the universality of the faith. And it is well to situate in this broader context those who would prefer the Catholic church with its rich traditions, impressive rituals and historical credentials, to be the kind of elite ghetto that for example Evelyn Waugh sometimes imagined the Roman church to be – a kind of other-world refuge for a literary or artistic elite, an extension of a cultured world where taste, temperament and type seem more important than faith, hope and love. But the simple faith of the common people (which is neither 'simple' nor 'common') should be unambiguously respected, for reasons I will explain. To aid this explanation I will situate my remarks against a background of verifiable faith-experiences, representative faith stances, a gallery of 'types' if you like, embellished somewhat with a medley of experience and invention, the remembered and the imagined. Not, I hasten to add, unvarnished pen-pictures of erstwhile parishioners, for leaving aside the recurring relevance of Pilate's great question, the truth in this instance is a variable commodity, fabled by the daughters of memory. The rationale for this approach finds an echo in Seamus Heaney's initial discovery of Patrick Kavanagh's poetry.[2] Suddenly on reading Kavanagh, Heaney's world became word:

> The barrels of blue potato-spray which had stood in my own childhood like holidays of pure colour in an otherwise grey field-day ... there they were standing their ground in print. [3]

Kavanagh gave him permission to dwell without cultural anxiety among the usual landmarks of his own life. My contention is that the unregarded data of the usual faith-life ... a mother telling her beads as she rocks her baby to sleep, a farmer blessing himself as the toll of an Angelus bell hangs in the summer air, a group of midday revellers doffing their hats as a hearse passes a pub, children racing the Stations of the Cross, a neighbour sitting in silent solidarity with a bereaved spouse after the excitement is over, a *meitheal* reacting to a local need ... merit, demand similar confirmation.

It is not that the horizons of the hills and fields of Mayo are to be sensed as the only or necessary horizons of faith-consciouness. Despite an understandable sense (feeling?) of *pietas* for Knock,

Croagh Patrick, Kilcummin *et al*, Mayo is not the whole world of God or faith or theology, but there is a sense in which ultimately it is the only world we know. We need to be brought back to where we belong, to dwell (if Heaney will pardon the paraphrase) without faith-anxiety among the landmarks of our own lives. The space we stand in has been emptied into us to keep. So it follows in a sense that the only theology we can credit is that which abjures the self-indulgence of academic impenetrability, but has an eye and an ear for the traces and sounds of God in the crannies of human experience and activity. Ultimately, for us in Mayo the only credible theologian is one who connects the great truths of Word and Sacrament with the lived experiences of Mayo people. There is a theology – there has to be a theology – that, like poetry, deals not so much with the expression of ideas but the relating of experiences and their explication through the prism of God's Word. A theology analogous to Michael Longley's peoms set in Mayo in which he tried:

> ...to put their district on the map
> And to name the fields for them.

God, St Teresa wrote, strolls amid the pots and pans. Or:

> Heaven in ordinarie, man well drest,
> The milkie way, the bird of Paradise
> ...something understood.[4]

For too long we have pressed our noses against the windowpanes of theology and have walked empty away. Our world needs to become Word.

Types: I: Maggie

I start with the experience of a woman from one extreme of the faith spectrum. Maggie is part of that loyal remnant scrupulously faithful to daily Mass. 'Attendance' would best describe her involvement in the lonely liturgy of her morning Eucharist. She opens the Church, covers her head with Pauline fervour, lights the altar candles, prepares the wine and water, drapes the amice at an agreeable distance from the single-bar heater in the sacristy to counteract the possibility that any suggestion of dampness on the nape of the celebrant's neck might render him indisposed. And in deference to the consistent absence of altar-boys, rings the Mass bell from her seat. During Mass, though invariably assuming the proper postures at appropriate times, she reads her own prayers from a black prayerbook breaking at the spine from a superfluity of memorial cards and leaflet devotions to a dizzying variety of saints, authentic, prospective and relegated. After Mass she performs the Stations of the Cross, lights complicated arrangements of shrine candles and votive lights and prays before every statue in the church.

In her innocent way, high levels of clerical sanctity are taken for granted on the false assumption that contact with holy things induces holiness by osmosis. Every clerical opinion receives such unrestrained affirmation that she could on occasion easily be mistaken for the nodding icon of Berganzi. Maggie is the clerical equivalent of the latter-day 'groupie', the devoted female fan who hangs around the edges of male pop stars. She is the unofficial secretary of 'Father's' fan-club. She would variously describe him as 'a nice man', 'a lovely priest', 'a saint'. No task is too menial to lessen the strain under which he is presumed to labour, no opportunity is lost to remind him of how busy he is, no detail of his uneventful life too unexciting to be endlessly remembered and repeated, no sock so worn as not to be lovingly darned to its original pristine condition, no opportunity too fleeting to avoid assuring him of how wonderful he is. Maggie combines at once such an irrepressible benignity of nature and such a fascination for the minutiae of clerical life that she presents as the Irish Catholic equivalent of Barbara Pym's 'Fine Women', the pious ladies who tend their begonias, ply the rector with gooseberry jam and fantasise after the curate.

II: Jack

Jack is a less benign species. He would share Maggie's faith constituency. The thick Sunday Missal, which he studiously carries with him, bears eloquent testimony to the importance he places on the religious dimension to life. Jack evinces that peculiar bullishness, endemic to pious people, that seeks to visit their individual personal truths on the rest of the human race. Jack is the recipient of a right-wing propagandist sheet, which escapes periodically from somewhere in Scotland, suggesting that the evils of the world and especially those besetting the church can be invariably traced to the radical propensities of either Darwin, Freud or Marx. Jack's agenda thereby receives fulsome confirmation and all kinds of imaginary windmills are tilted at ... the advent of lay ministers of the Eucharist, the gimmickry of the modern liturgy, rampant sexual promiscuity and so on. There is about Jack that dark Manichean inclination to postulate evil in whatever is not immediately reconcilable with his narrow, myopic view of life. The worries of the world are written all over his face, that constantly concerned look usually associated with grief or haemorrhoids.

III: Michael

Michael has a different perspective. The nearest he gets to Mass is the back porch where he folds his arms and displays a studied disregard for the proceedings. The whole point of his demeanour is to establish a certain agnostic distance from, if not rejection of, the ritual. Michael would sympathise with Updike's view that churches bore the same relation to God as bill-boards did to Coca-Cola, promoting thirst without actually quenching it. The past for him is a foreign country and, even though he continues to defer to the social conventions of religious practice, it is an increasingly empty ritual. For him there is no detectable difference between believer and unbeliever. The rituals of Word and Sacrament are a kind of verbal music. The presence of a priest still confusingly reassuring – in Heaney's words:

> Something in them would be ratified
> when they saw you at the door in your black suit
> arriving like some kind of holy mascot. [5]

IV: Leo

Leo, on the other hand, has no such philosophical doubts. Not a man given to weighing the great metaphysical questions, he spends most mornings in bed, most afternoons watching television and most nights in a licensed establishment playing darts and consuming vast quantities of alcoholic beverage. His income derives from the proceeds of an illicit distillery, unemployment assistance with a generous moiety in respect of the bevy of offspring he has, with his reluctant spouse so assiduously propagated, and irregular excusions into what we call 'the black economy'. Leo could be described as one of the great supports of his local church or, more precisely, the back wall of his local church with which he has over the years developed a special affinity. The extent of his religious commitment is a vague presence in the vicinity of Sunday worship during which he is more liable to buy turf than to say prayers. Extraneous religious matters are the natural concern of his harrassed spouse who, when not presiding with spectacular ineptitude over the tumult inflicted on the household by an indefinite number of offspring, is sampling the delights of bingo in the nearest market-town, or whatever alternative social occasion warrants an excuse for getting out of the house.

V: Pat

Pat needs to get out of the house too but for very different reasons. A reluctant bachelor, he returned from England to care for ageing parents who disobliged his marriage prospects by surviving into their eighties. By then the girls he had 'walked out with' were either married in Kent or waitressing in Hampstead. Time or fate or God had predestined the unfortunate series of events that condemned him to looking into a lonely pint of Guinness every night of the week and finding his reluctant feet in the kind of bitter subculture Eugene McCabe captured so vividly in 'King of the Castle'.

Pat is a man without a past or a future. After several pints he can be coaxed into mulling over the experience of what Kavanagh called 'the purgatory of middle-aged virginity' and the emotional and sexual deprivation that attends it. At Mass every Sunday, Patrick is no reluctant observer, savouring as he does the richness of the ritual, understanding through it something of the majesty and mystery of God and yet declining the invitation to God's table apart from the annual Easter duty on Trinity Sunday after a careful confession in Knock the day before.

VI: George

George on the other hand attends and communicates every Sunday. It would be unthinkable not to do so, a betrayal of an ancestral loyalty. Sunday worship is an act of solidarity with the community, a revered tradition validated by unbroken habit and the blood of martyrs. George is strong on loyalty ... to the GAA where he refuses to defer to the growing popularity of 'other codes', avoiding any undue familiarity with 'foreign' games that might compromise the athletic purity of 'the Gael' ... to Fianna Fáil, where phrases like 'soldiers of destiny' and 'the natural party of government' are remorselessly employed to deflect any deviation from what de Valera saw when he looked into his own heart ... to the Roman Catholic church, where his conservative disposition and allegiance to tradition find a comfortable home. George is of course also a Pioneer, a Legionary of Mary, a caller of bingo numbers, a bearer of clerical water, a hewer of clerical wood and a multiplicity of menial tasks for the execution of which over the years clergy tend to develop a somewhat restrained proclivity. It may be churlish to say so, but George is also (let it be said) a veritable pain in the neck in that there is no crevice in his unimaginative mind through which even the merest glimmer of compromise might possibly filter. It was for someone like him that Helder Camara wrote the words:

> Teach your child from infancy
> to love open spaces
> Widen his mind
> He will be glad of this
> especially if later
> he must endure
> a life confined
> by a slit window's littleness
> to one small patch of sky.

George's slit window is for him a boon not a limitation. His truth can be contained within rigid boundaries and beyond that any unnecessary freedom to postulate alternatives simply confuses. For him – whatever about Newman's terse injunction – to live well is not to change at all.

This gallery of 'types' is not of course complete but is sufficient for my purposes here. 'A 'faith' is a factor common to all these types. But I wonder whether I can use the word 'simple' or even 'religious' to describe it. From outside – and an outside perspective is the only perspective I can have – it looks like a faith without freedom.

The Pagan Influence

The faith is a common perspective, inherited and embraced, through which meaning is found, purpose revealed, mystery unmasked with ritual and rubric, Word and Sacrament. It is of course Christian in that it draws on a collective memory, rich in image and symbol, the result of an ongoing process that is the product of centuries of selective assimilation under the twin leavens of Scripture and tradition. But the roots of this common perspective predate Bethlehem and Calvary. Though the word 'pagan' is inaccurate, because it pays scant regard to the dynamic of selection, discrimination and assimilation that parent tradition, it will do.

The roots of this common perspective stretch back into pagan times. The effort to situate a life-boat service near Belmullet had less to do with economic or political difficulties in providing a seaworthy vessel, than with the popular dogma among Erris fishermen that regardless the sea would invariably claim a victim. The custom too is not to touch hawthorn:

> Not to bring it indoors for the sake of the luck
> such constraint would forfeit –
> a child might die, perhaps, or an unexplained
> fever speckle heifers.[6]

What Eavan Boland calls from the vantage point of the present, 'the superstitious aura of hawthorn', the sprinkling of the blood of a cock on the four corners of the house on St Martin's night to keep evil spirits away, and other similar 'traditions', are all part of the baggage of this common perspective. The special 'office' of the alcoholic priest resonates with a cultural distrust of the treatment of the individual by great institutions; the gathering motif of the Eucharist echoes the ritual of the *Aonach*, the symbolic coming together of the tribe; *Lá an Logha* in Belmullet on the 15th August has less to do with the Feast of the Assumption than the visitation of sacred and originally pagan places. The pilgrimage to the top of the hill, we now call Croagh Patrick, predates the visitation of our national saint and was *Cruachán Aigle*, the mountain sacred to our pagan ancestors. And the recent upsurge of 'green consciousness', expressed so beautifully in the celebrated oration attributed to

Chief Seattle,[7] represents in rural Irish terms a modern echo of the earth goddess *Cailleach*. There is beneath the texture of Irish rural life, an accretion between paganism and Christianity that defines the common perspective.

The Clerical Factor

Another defining factor has been the all-pervading influence of a definitively clerical culture and the ethos of control that pervaded it. The form of Catholicism that James Joyce experienced in Dublin as antipathetic and inimical to the literary imagination, distrustful of independent thought, suspicious of novelty, indifferent to beauty and fearful of sexuality, spawned the clerical culture that in rural Ireland, and not least in Mayo, spread its controlling tentacles into every area of community and personal concern. It seemed that every book, every decision, every thought almost had to receive official clerical imprimatur. The writer Aidan C. Matthews called it 'a world of surveillance',[8] the Big Brother syndrome on less organised but no less effective scale. Young curates, with the oil of ordination scarcely dry on their hands, ranted at their unfortunate flocks, often berating them for imagined or imaginary sins – ranting that said less about the quality of their people's lives than their own fanaticisms.

Their seniors meanwhile, often with the aid of definitively curious housekeepers, took a longer view and held their considerable fire for the occasional recalcitrant individual who indicated a worrying propensity for anarchy, by suggesting for example that even though St Patrick's Day invariably fell during Lent, it might be possible to hold a dance if the proceeds were directed towards parochial funds. And their long-suffering people, the unwilling (though not unwitting) recipients of a great deal of unsolicited advice on matters clearly extraneous to whatever individual or vocational expertise their clerical superiors might claim, more often than not simply kept their heads down in mystified silence, wondering around many a hob, what particular personality trait or psychic idiosyncrasy condemned apparently intelligent men to such irrational, even bizarre, presumption. The P.P., deciding what play would be staged, at what times and to what groups the local hall would be available, when dances would be held and what bands would play, who would or would not play full-forward in the divisional final and so on, seems in retrospect an exaggeratedly comic reconstruction of Mayo rural life in the past. But those of us who were there recognise only too well, not just the denial of individual and personal freedom such rampant clerical authoritarianism entailed, but the attendant insidious oppression that stultified individuals on communal growth. Frank O'Connor remarked in the fifties that an 'Irishman's private life began at Holyhead', and Nuala O'Faolain's theory that even now the emigrant ship receives an impetus from the desire to flee the oppressive confines of Irish life, is not far wide of the mark.[9] The redeeming influence of individual clerics, or spurious notions of loyalty to the clerical caste, should not compromise the naming of this lamentable reality.

It seems inconceivable with hindsight that the prevailing clerical wisdom of the day was not just uncritically ingested but vigorously defended to the last detail. Atheism or agnosticism, even in the most compunctious form, received the full brunt of Sheehan's 'proofs' for the existence of God, which, in deference to the prevailing philosophical wisdom of the day, were offered almost as revealed truth, even though to maintain them demanded several irrational quantum leaps. There was a sense that belief could crumble if the particular philosophical tradition that spawned these proofs was not indiscriminately defended – a bad case of the philosophical tail wagging the theological dog! The importance of Latin in the liturgy was unambiguously defended on whatever specious grounds were current at the time. Nevertheless celebrants galloped disedifyingly through the Mass, and struggled uncomprehendingly through the Holy Week ceremonies, while their congregations said Rosaries to pass the time. Women wearing slacks while receiving Communion were perceived as a form of moving blasphemy, and intolerable aberrations in public. Professors of Canon Law in the pages of the *Irish Ecclesiastical Record* (now mercifully defunct) dealt with the more bizarre pastoral imponderables placed at their hallowed feet by the clerical foot-soldiers in the trenches – whether for example the wearing of the mantilla (a black lace scarf popularised by its fashionable use at Hollywood funerals) fulfilled the Pauline injunction on women covering their heads.

It was the time of course before truth was paid the courtesy of a sense of hierarchy. Yet it remains incomprehensible how a whole generation of highly intelligent men could indiscriminately defend such untenable positions, without any apparent sense of intellectual or personal compromise. The reason went deeper than the irascibility endemic to the clerical state (exacerbated by celibacy or over-exposure to unruly altar-boys and overly pious women). We can now see that men of authoritarian temperament were drawn to the priesthood like moths to a night-light. There was nothing to prevent unquestioned and unchallenged clerical authority becoming infallible insight into what was best for lay people. The inevitable and untimely debilitating corollary to this was the human tendency to tolerate the foibles and pander to the eccentricities of those in positions of power. When that power was associated with access to God and the removal of sin, on which eternal happiness or punishment may attend, it dissuaded any conceivable 'Oliver' from even the merest suggestion of dissent.

What David Lodge, the Catholic novelist (if such a term means anything anymore) called 'the suffocating embrace of mother Church' was, to my gallery of types, similarly perceived as oppressive. Even Maggie, normally embarrassingly sychophantic to the clergy, would on occasions voice reservations about being rusticated in a former existence from the Children of Mary because of an uncharacteristic bout of company-keeping. Jack would harbour resentments about clerically-controlled decision-making. Leo would object to the lack of financial accountability. Pat would blame the denial of the sensual, the distrust of passion that allowed a celibate clergy to pander to their own narrow obsessions. George would resent the ill-disguised efforts to influence political decisions. Even though external practice – public deferral to at least minimal observance – was the *sine qua non* for, and in the absence of an alternative ideology or the freedom to pursue it, the prevailing wisdom, the common perspective, the faith-stance had a sense of general oppression as its darker shadow.

By say 1950, the sense of oppressiveness was widespread. There were six times more priests in Ireland than a hundred years earlier. The church was a dynamic, expanding institution (health, welfare, education) in a dead economy. The Roman policy of rigid uniformity was ruthlessly efficient. But the difference between 1950 and 1990 is not four decades but eternity. The social and religious cohesion of Irish life is beginning to crumble. The influences of the media, particularly television, the ease of foreign travel, the economic boom of the sixties followed by the depression of the late seventies and the emigration haemorrhage of the eighties, set in difficult relief the unexamined certainties of the past. After twenty years of Northern violence, the old Gaelic nationalist ideals seem peculiarly inadequate as an acceptable ethos for a new Ireland. After twenty years of savouring, even in carefully measured portions, the freedoms promised by the Second Vatican Council, the old clerical authoritarianism and its oppressive shadow seem particularly inadequate to meet our religious needs.

The young have distanced themselves from the old agenda and are mesmerised if not repelled by desperate efforts to keep alive a form of Catholicism to which they cannot assent. Obsessions with intellectual adherance to a body of dogma, denunciations of materialism and injunctions to remain faithful to the devotional food of the past appear as pointless efforts to keep out the tide when it might be more helpful to encourage people to learn to swim in the new waters.[10] Traditional dogma has to make its peace with a modern ethos of freedom and tolerance. The heretofore placidity of the more agreeable daughters of Eve has given way to an impression that women are quite a different species. For instance, promoting the traditional image of Mary as a model for women is interpreted as at best insensitive, at worst sinister, ignoring as it does a quite separate feminist agenda, ruthlessly at odds with the male-dominated antediluvianism of the past. Priests uneasy with anything less than absolute servility have become more familiar with their own finitude and are now regularly reminded that they are mortal. The erstwhile universal put-down 'I'm the parish priest' has been relegated to a synonym for negativity, if not an unacceptable insularity. The clerical culture that facilitated the oppressiveness of Irish rural life is falling apart. The past is now a foreign country. It is no longer possible to disabuse the young of their novel notions by worrying sermons on hell-fire, or feminists of their perceived heresies by toasting them over a low flame. It would be delusory to suggest that Maggie or Jack or Pat have read themselves into a personal appreciation of Metz's 'Theology of the World' or Moltmann's 'Theology of Hope', or are avaricious for seminars on Teilhard de Chardin. But new thoughts, ideas, perspectives on personal freedom, have percolated even to the confined faith-worlds they inhabit. Even George no longer wishes to play a part in a drama written by someone else a long time ago. In clerical circles the words 'Vatican Two' may be 'overworn', as Feste might say in *Twelfth Night*, but among God's people in Mayo there is a *féar gorta* for the freedom they conjured up.

Whether the clergy of Mayo and of the wider church are prepared to trust the hunger of their people for personal freedom; whether they are willing – or indeed able – to walk alongside their people into an uncertain future, is a different matter. It requires an extraordinary maturity for a priest to divest himself of caste authority. It requires even greater maturity to learn the new skills, to develop the deeper sensitivity that will facilitate the partnership that the Council Fathers encouraged. And not least it requires deep faith and an inner freedom in the priest himself, to set out into the threatening waters of the future. It will be difficult to avoid the temptation of forever heading back to the more sheltered harbours of the past, to disown the individual voyages in favour of the settled route. It will be difficult to live with the constant fear that the faith-experience of Mayo will end up, in Philip Larkin's words as:

That vast moth-eaten musical brocade
Created to pretend we never die. [11]

Yet it is a risk that we cannot afford not to take.

Notes
1. McDonagh, Enda, *Gift and Call*, Dublin, Gill and Macmillan, 1975, p 4.
2. Heaney, Seamus, *The Government of the Tongue*, Faber 1988.
2. Heaney, ibid. p 7.
4. Gardner, Helen (Ed.), *The Metaphysical Poets*, Penguin 1971, p. 124 from 'Prayer' by George Herbert.
5. Heaney, Seamus, *Station Island*, Faber 1984, 'Station Island' p 702.
6. Boland, Eavan, 'White Hawthorn in the West of Ireland', published in *The Irish Times* on 24.6.89.
7. Letter of Chief Seattle to Washington quoted in *The Christian Way Series*, part 3, p 39, Ray Brady, Veritas Publications.
8. *The Irish Times* on 2.12.88.
9. *The Furrow*, March 1989.
10. McRedmond, Louis in *The Church Now*, Edited John Cumming & Paul Burns, Gill and Macmillan, 1980.
11. Larkin, Philip, 'Aubade' in *Times Literary Supplement*, 23.12.77.

Power or Empowerment?
– A Woman's Perspective

Ben Kimmerling

In 1986 a synod on the laity was held in Rome. In 1988, as a follow up to this, Pope John Paul II issued a post-synodal document, *The Vocation and Mission of the Laity*. One of the principal themes running through that document is that of the church as community, a community where the dignity of each individual is respected, where the basic equality of every Christian is recognised. I believe such a community would of necessity be one which had moved beyond lay/clerical distinctions and the stratification which these distinctions imply. It is however painfully obvious that such a community of equals does not exist in the church at the present time. It seems to me that one of the factors inhibiting its development is the legacy of clericalism which today's priests have unwittingly, and often reluctantly, inherited from the past.

In this article I look at one aspect of clericalism, namely clerical power. I suggest that, in the light of the post-synodal document, clerical power is a power which should be diminishing, while priestly power – whether exercised by men as it is now, or perhaps eventually by women – is a power which can endure.

Prior to Vatican II the relationship of the clergy with the laity was (for reasons outside the scope of this article) one of extreme inequality. The clergy were paternalistic. The laity were dependent. However, as a result of the Council's insights into the role and mission of the laity, that relationship has now begun to evolve. But this evolution is not going very smoothly. There appear to be many disturbances along the way. So I am trying to understand not only what's going on in the hearts of the laity during these disturbances, but to understand what might be happening in the hearts of the clergy as well.

As a Christian I have been deeply influenced by the insights of Vatican II. So naturally when I became a mother (of now almost grown-up children) I found it necessary to continually re-examine, in the light of these new insights, the traditional notions concerning parental authority which I had inherited as a Catholic from my Mayo foremothers. When I look at the clergy of Mayo and elsewhere, who have, like myself, inherited traditional notions of authority, I see them struggling, too, to apply the councils insights to their relationship with the laity. So as parent and as priest we can perhaps listen to one another's experience as we struggle to find new ways of exercising authority.

From my feminine/parental perspective I see certain similarities between the evolution of my own relationship with my children over the past twenty-two years and the evolving relationship of the clergy with the laity since the Council. One similarity lies in the fact that both the clergy and myself exercise facilitative power in relation to our respective partners. My parental task is to facilitate the growth of my children so that they may become mature human beings. The clergy's task is to facilitate the growth of the laity so that they may become mature Christians. So we both, by virtue of our roles, are in positions of power – a power/authority which Christians believe to be God-given.

Yet another similarity is to be found in the pattern of disturbance which at times seems to be common to both relationships. I believe that the disturbances in both cases are associated with the issues of authority and power.

In view of these similarities, I have begun to wonder whether a useful, though admittedly limited, parallel might not be drawn between these two sets of experiences, i.e. that of a parent in relation to a growing child and that of the clergy in relation to a maturing laity.[1] So while keeping the clergy/laity relationship in the back of our minds, let us look at the way in which a parent's relationship with a child evolves, in order: (1) to clarify how facilitative power works; (2) to identify abuses of that power; and (3) to discern what disturbances in that relationship are all about.

(I write of the parent as mother because I have personal experience of mothering. But I presume what I say could apply to fathering too.)

Parent/Child Relationship

When a mother first meets her new born son[2] there is a gross imbalance of power in their relationship with one another. The son is virtually powerless, i.e. he lacks the power to make any decisions for himself. The mother on the other hand has awesome power. She has personal power which she uses to make decisions on her own behalf. In addition she has parental power which she uses to make decisions on behalf of her child. This latter power is the focus of the present article. So let us home in on the parent/child relationship in order to see this facilitative parental power at work.

Parental Power

When parenting begins the mother holds decision-making power in trust for her son, rather as a guardian might hold money in trust for a ward until such time as the ward is old enough to use it responsibly him/herself. One of the mother's tasks as parent is to create an environment within which this decision-making power – this power-in-trust – which she temporarily holds, can be handed over gradually to the child. This handing over must be done at a pace and in a manner which allows the child to experience the availability of this decision-making power, to freely appropriate his own life. So through this gradual handing over of his decision-making power, the mother facilitates the child's growth. And if the process goes smoothly, the child will eventually become a responsible and decisive human being, who will be able to relate in equality with other human beings including, of course, his mother.

This seems to me somewhat like the task which faces the clergy in relation to the laity, if the post-Vatican II church is to become a community of equals and lay people are to assume their full and equal responsibility as mature Christians in the church.

Early Childhood

At the very beginning of the parental relationship the child is completely helpless. So the mother has the power to make all the decisions on his behalf. Even during the early years she still has the power to make most of the decisions, though she does hand over a little bit of decision-making power, in certain areas, to the child, e.g. she gives him the freedom to decide what he will do in certain safe places, what games he will play with certain safe toys etc. As the child begins to grow she has to decide at each successive stage, to give new freedom – to let go a little more decision-making power – to the child. She has to discern what is the correct amount of power to release on each occasion, e.g. whether the child is ready to make his own decisions about the clothes he will wear, the books he will read, the friends he will make, the schools he will attend etc. All of these freedoms, which are limited and carefully controlled by the mother, give the child the opportunity to make increasingly complex and responsible decisions about his own life.

So during this phase of the relationship, the mother controls the distribution of decision-making power to her son. It is important that she gets this distribution right. Too much power will confuse the child. Too little will constrict his growth. Yet all the time the mother, while trying to teach the child and protect him from danger, must remember that some day that child will have to become an independent and decisive human being in his own right.

If in early childhood the mother gets this task of handing over decision-making power fairly right on most occasions - i.e. if the new balance of power, which is established in the relationship after each successive share-out, is appropriate to that stage of the child's development – then the child begins to grasp the connection between responsible decision-making and growth. Though he is quite unable to articulate this notion, nevertheless it becomes an important part of the child's lived experience. Consequently, if he is allowed, he begins instinctively to seek out decision-making experiences for himself, e.g. he may express a desire to travel alone by bus or to bake a cake unsupervised. When the mother listens sensitively to these desires, they help her to discern the areas in which the child is ready to grow. So her discernment of his needs does not take place in a vacuum. She constantly receives pointers from him. And if experiences of decision-making are present fairly consistently in his early life, a sense of personal freedom and personal responsibility soon begin to manifest themselves in his growing personality. In this way, a sense of his own dignity as a person begins to develop and an important cornerstone of his mature personality is gradually laid down.

Empowering the Laity – A Beginning
Since Vatican II many of the clergy have been engaged in a somewhat similar process. They have redistributed some decision-making power to the laity by giving them responsibility in certain areas of church life, e.g. in giving pre-marriage courses etc. These experiences of responsibility and the opportunities they provide for lay decision-making, though limited and carefully controlled by the clerical authorities, have nevertheless enabled some lay people to have good experiences of decision-making in the Christian community. Such people have begun to see a connection between these experiences of decision-making and their own spiritual growth. Having had a taste of the fulfilment which flows from responsible decision-making, they have now become eager for more. But discernment of lay people's needs should not take place in a vacuum. If the clergy listen sensitively to the desires expressed by these committed lay people they will indicate the areas in which the laity need new freedom to grow.

The freedom and the responsibility which lay people have already been granted, have enabled them to discover latent ministerial talent in themselves. And they have come to believe in the possibility of other lay ministries which are either still undiscovered or are not yet officially recognised. This active participation by lay people in the life of the Christian community has given many of them an increased sense of belonging to the church, of being co-responsible for it – and even perhaps, a sense of co-ownership of it. They are now increasingly aware of their personal freedom and personal responsibility as Christians. And many of them are deeply committed to promoting the vocation and mission of the laity in the church. The official church has therefore very successfully set in motion a power-sharing process which, by allowing greater freedom for lay decision-making, is gradually empowering lay people, enhancing their sense of their own dignity as Christians and promoting their growth.

From Control to Trust

In the parent/child relationship this process of redistributing power from mother to child usually goes fairly smoothly during the early years. The gradual letting go of power by the mother is responded to by the gradual claiming of it by the child. So the balance of power in the relationship is changing all the time. The nature of the relationship is changing too. The child is being controlled less and trusted more. There are many areas of control which the mother is relieved to let go, e.g. she is glad when she can trust the child to walk to and from school on his own, instead of having to accompany him every day. This letting go of power from mother to son gives each of them new feeedoms which they welcome and enjoy. Normally at this stage of the relationship, these small moves from control to trust are initiated by the mother. And she experiences a keen sense of satisfaction and fulfilment when, as a result of her own free decision to transfer power, a consequent growth of trust occurs.

Occasionally the child may create a disturbance if he seeks new freedom prematurely. But the mother can usually postpone granting it by redirecting his attention to more appropriate activities until he grows a little more mature. So she withholds power at this stage simply for the good of the child. Such rows do not unduly disturb the mother. She knows that she has a monopoly of power. She doesn't mind sharing out of this abundance. And when she does share some power with him, she still feels very comfortably in control.

Trusting the Laity

I imagine that there are many parish priests and curates who feel the same satisfaction and fulfilment as the mother, when they trust lay people to plan liturgies, to counsel married couples etc. This redistribution of power was initiated by the free decision of the clergy. It was responded to with enthusiasm by the laity. So this initial move from control to trust is a source of satisfaction and fulfilment for both. It promotes the growth of the laity while at the same time easing the workload of priests, thereby giving them a little more freedom to follow other priestly pursuits. At the same time, because the clergy still have a monopoly of power, because they are sharing power out of their abundance, this limited and controlled transfer of power poses no serious threat to clerical authority or role.

Balancing Needs

The mother has a great deal of control over the child's freedom during the first decade or so of his life. It is largely she who decides what his needs are. And it is she who, in the last analysis, decides whether or not these needs should be met. But in making her assessment of his needs, she is also in a position to take account of her own needs. This means that she has the task of discerning the relative importance of both sets of needs, of prioritising them and then of distributing his freedom and decision-making power in accordance with this assessment. Of course as a loving mother, she strikes an unselfish balance between his needs and her own. This in effect probably means giving him more freedom than is comfortable for himself. For example it may mean giving him the freedom to play with water when he is a toddler even though she has to mop up the mess; or giving him the freedom to climb in the mountains when he's older, even though this may cause a certain amount of anxiety for herself.

But in addition to a willingness to suffer discomfort and inconvenience in order to promote her son's growth, a mother has to be prepared to allow his existence to challenge her in an even more fundamental way. A family, like any other group of people who form a community, structure their communal life in particular ways. They do so in order to preserve the meaning, harmony and continuity of family life from one generation to the next. Some examples of these communal structures would be – certain ritual celebrations, certain objects, traditions, habits, titles, certain styles of dress, rules of conduct and modes of thought. Any or all of these maybe of immense importance to the mother – for instance, the rituals surrounding the celebration of Christmas, or the tradition of the eldest son following the father's profession or trade. Indeed if her life has been constructed around these, she may even assume that they are of ultimate importance! But these structures were established to meet the needs of her own or previous generations. So the value of each of them must be reassessed in the light of the needs of a new generation. When weighed against the need of her son to exist and to flourish, the present importance of these structures will be revealed: structures which she had previously assumed to be of ultimate importance may be seen to be of only relative importance instead. So in order to promote her flourishing she becomes willing to let go many of these old structures which up till then, gave meaning, shape and purpose to her life. Indeed if she is not willing to let go of them when necessary, she is denying him existence. She is in a real sense denying him life!

Abuse of Parental Power

It is clear that a mother has the power to put her own self-centred concerns before the developmental needs of her son. In doing so she not only stunts his life but she stunts the life of the community to which they both belong. She might do this for a variety of reasons; because she is unwilling to sacrifice her own comfort even for the sake of her son; or because she considers the preservation of established structures to be more important than the flourishing of a human being. Or she might do it because she is fearful and insecure and thus unable to trust; or because she is inordinately fond of power and so she wants to keep her son permanently dependent in order to maintain her own position of dominance. In all of these situations, she is giving a higher priority to control than to trust. But whenever a mother subordinates the value of trust to that of control for any of these self-centred reasons, she abuses her parental authority and power.

The power to balance needs, the power to promote or inhibit the flourishing of another human being, lies at the very heart of the parental relationship. I believe that it lies at the heart of the clerical/lay relationship too.

Abuse of Clerical Power

Like the mother, the clergy too can chose to put their own self-centred concerns before the developmental needs of the laity. They can do so for exactly the same reasons as the mother – out of selfishness as in the case of 'bachelor priests' who don't want to disturb their own comfortable lives; or out of a false notion that certain church structures are more important than the flourishing of human beings. Certain rituals, objects, traditions, titles, habits, styles of dress, ways of relating, rules of conduct and modes of thought, may be of immense importance to some clergy. Indeed if they have constructed their lives around them, these structures may even seem to be of ultimate importance! However when the structures which have been established by past generations are counterbalanced against the need of a new generation of lay people to flourish within the Christian community, what previously seemed to be of ultimate importance may be revealed to be of merely relative importance. So the clergy, like the mother, are challenged in the most fundamental way by the emergent laity and by their need to flourish. Like the mother, they too must be prepared to let go of many of the old structures which, until now, have given meaning, shape and purpose to their lives.

The clergy may also inhibit the flourishing of the laity because fear and insecurity make them unable to trust. Or they may have an inordinate love of power. So they may try to keep the laity dependent, in order to maintain their own position of dominance. To subordinate trust to control for any of these motives, is, I believe, an abuse of clerical power.

But this abuse of power is usually neither deliberate nor consciously chosen. The deeply buried motives which cause it may not even be accessible to the individual her/himself. But buried motives can be brought into consciousness by the protest of someone else. And thereby they become the subject of reflection and of deliberate choice. Of course protest causes disturbance in a relationship. But disturbance isn't always a bad thing. Indeed, because it moves a person beyond habitual responses into the area of discernment and choice, it can even be a call to conversion.

Returning to the parental relationship let us look at a situation where disturbance surfaces the buried motives of the mother and the doing so actually brings conversion about.

Disturbance and Power Struggles

During the teenage years the son grows increasingly independent. Eventually his stock of power almost equals the mother's own. He now feels the urge to push out the boundaries of his own freedom, not just in relation to the world of books, clothes etc. but in relation to people too, especially in relation to authority figures like his mother. But during these years he also grows in complexity. He becomes more unique, more opaque and mysterious. So in spite of the mother's goodwill and sincere efforts of discernment, she now frequently fails to anticipate or even recognise her son's hidden needs. However the boy himself has been growing in self-awareness and is now much more in touch with his own inner being. He feels an increased urge to participate in his own history, to take steps to identify and meet his own needs. He wants to take over control of his own destiny. And though he may not be able to put this idea into coherent language, he does try to put it into action. While previously his mother discerned his needs and granted him power, now he is discerning his own needs and setting out to meet them. So he seems to be grabbing power while aggressively proclaiming that this power is by right his own.

Very frequently the mother is taken by surprise and is hurt by his behaviour. She becomes angry and indignant. And she refuses to let the power go. So power struggles become a feature of the relationship. And no matter what superficial issue sparks off the conflict, in the long run these disturbances are all about the same thing, namely, does the mother who has always been in charge of the distribution of decision-making power, any longer have the right to exercise this kind of control? Her son clearly doesn't think so. He insists that she must trust him. She insists on her right to control.

God Given Power or Clerical Control?

In the church there are many examples of this type of power struggle at all levels from the local parish upwards. Perhaps the most obvious example is the power struggle which centres on the issue of contraception. In this case the official church authorities have discerned the needs of married people and have arrived at one set of conclusions. However many married people have done their own discerning and have arrived at quite a different set of conclusions. So now these married Christians are 'grabbing' the power to make decisions based on their own discerning while aggressively claiming that this power is by right their own.

This and similar protests on the part of lay people, (whether women, sisters, parish councils, or other lay groups,) have caused many clergy to agonise about the nature and limits of clerical authority – in somewhat the same way as the Christian mother has to agonise about the limits of her parental authority. So perhaps it will help if we look at the circumstances which raise this question for her and at the conclusions to which her agonising leads.

The Questions Surface
At the teenage stage of the parental relationship, the mother and son seem to have their own views on almost every issue. They are not necessarily in agreement, so serious disturbances continue to occur. These are not the minor and unequal skirmishes of early childhood but intensely painful and deadly serious struggles – struggles which the mother is by no means guaranteed to win. And, for a while, winning can seem all important. Because now that her son is so decisive and opinionated, the mother feels in real danger of losing parental control.

But how could her son manage without her guidance? How could he decide what's right if she doesn't retain her controlling parental role? Surely he's not implying she's redundant! Without her role as parent what purpose, what meaning would her life have any more?

She can see only two alternatives, either redundancy – which she finds totally unacceptable – or the reimposiition of parental control. So she enters into battle with great righteousness, determined to quell anarchy, to impose her authority, to defend and preserve her parental role. She decides to issue a clearly worded ultimatum. 'I am your mother. I have God-given parental authority. Therefore you have got to obey.'

But her opponent is equally determined. He feels that his freedom, his future, his dignity as a person, have to be defended too. So he retaliates with another ultimatum. 'I now have the right and responsibility to make my own decisions. Either you trust me or I won't hang around here anymore!' In the disturbance which ensues, she is most painfully defeated because her son squares up to her and absolutely refuses to yield.

Agonising
She withdraws to lick her wounds and do some thinking, to review her assumptions and see where she goes from here. As she reflects on the various lessons she has learned, she finds that pain has

been, as usual, an efficient teacher. She's learned that she can't impose authority on an unwilling recipient. She can't enforce obedience or dominate the spirit of a now independent son. This son must be respected, never driven. She can't prolong his dependence to suit her own needs. She can't take back the power she has given nor control the way that power will be used.

She realises with a degree of chagrin that in using his decision-making power, he is only doing what she has always encouraged him to do. But she hadn't foreseen that he'd use it like this! In relation to herself! Yet perhaps that too should have been expected. Because after all, though she may be his mother, her opinions are not always or necessarily correct. Indeed because she is human and a woman, even her most deeply held convictions, which she thought indisputable, maybe merely a partial and sexually conditioned perspective on a larger and ever-evolving truth. So perhaps the time has come now when, in her own search for truth, she must listen to and take into account his masculine perspective. And she must trust that he likewise will take the feminine perspective into account, as he freely seeks out that larger Truth for himself.

And after all hasn't she spent all these years training him to be decisive? Didn't she rear him for independence? Doesn't she in her heart of hearts want him to be free? Free even of herself? Yes! And of all unexamined or imposed assumptions? Yes! Free to conduct his own search for Truth without coercion from her. So she has not after all given birth to a monster. No! It is only her chickens – her deeply held convictions about personal freedom – which are at last coming home to roost. She understands now that the process of responsible decision-making, which she herself so carefully set in motion, has gathered momentum and is merely being carried through to its logical conclusion by her son.

She begins to realise that this son, who won't be bullied, will listen to reason, that he can be trusted though he cannot be controlled. She concedes that she has no monopoly on wisdom, he seems to have a wisdom of his own. After all it was he who saw the need for confrontation. He even picked a time when she might learn. He instinctively knew that she would have to suffer, before he could claim his power and stand alone. Somehow he knew that a community of equals doesn't just happen – it's something which, through the striving and suffering of both sides, has to be achieved.

She sees now that she can't preserve her old role as parent without contradicting all that she has lived by over the years. He must have his freedom even though it means radically redefining her own role. And so she relinquishes her identity as parent, accepts the challenge of her new freedom, believes that her teaching, if true, will remain relevant, and trustingly lets go those last vestiges of power to her son. Obsolescence she concludes is built into the very nature of the parental relationship![3]

Becoming a Community of Equals
The time had come for this mother when, instead of continuing to be solely her child's teacher, she had, for a while at least, to humbly allow herself to be taught. She had to be taught that her son had become her equal. This required a complete and unanticipated shattering of ingrained habits and responses, a reversal of long established procedures. So a major emotional and intellectual upheaval was required in order to bring about this realisation and to see its logical consequences. But it's doubtful if she could ever have learned this painful lesson without the help of her son! It was only when her emotional comfort was severely disturbed by his protest, that she was driven to face those difficult and awkward questions within herself. Disturbance surfaced questions which complacency couldn't even touch. Disturbance was in fact a call to conversion! [4]

This shattering of the mother's assumption that she, the parent, is the final source of wisdom is extremely painful, because it heralds the 'death' of her child: he must die as a child in order to be reborn as a man. Because if the old childish way of relating isn't abandoned, if the unequal structure of the relationship isn't questioned, if the son's equality isn't somehow made explicit – then a new adult relationship based on that equality will never be brought about.

Maybe there's a need for agonising and 'death' in the clergy/laity relationship too? Because if the old childish way of relating to the clergy isn't abandoned, if the unequal structure of that relationship isn't questioned, if the basic equality of lay Christians isn't somehow made explicit, then a more mature relationship based on that equality will never be put in place.

Both mothers and clergy share power, at first out of a position of abundance; so the early stages of a facilitative relationship are relatively easy for us. Our power-sharing – like many such gestures of generosity – poses no threat to our position of superiority, yet it does give us a sense of satisfaction and fulfilment. Indeed it can even induce a certain self-satisfied glow! But essentially we are giving because it suits us. That's why we have no difficulty going that first mile!

However, real power-sharing is about going the second mile. It's about giving when it doesn't suit us; giving when our partner's power has built up to threatening proportions and our own stock of parental/clerical power has reached an all-time low. At this stage, when son or laity demand still more power, we are extremely reluctant to let our last bit of parental/clerical power go. Because that's the bit that makes the difference! That's the bit that maintains our superiority, that confers advantage, that gives us power of veto. Yet if we are genuinely committed to equality we must be prepared to let that last significant bit of controlling power go.

As a son receives, appropriates and uses the decision-making power which the mother redistributes, it is transformed into his own personal power. When this hand-over is complete, the mother is completely divested of parental power. From then on mother and son relate to one another as mature and equal adults – each out of her/his own personal power.

The personal power of a committed adult Christian is exercised and further developed as that person strives to live the Truth. It is a power which can endure because it comes from within the person rather than from any particular office or role. This is the power upon which relationships of equality must be based.

Parental power on the other hand is a decision-making power which is to be exercised sensitively on behalf of the child. It is a controlling power, a facilitating power, a benevolent power. But it is a temporary power. And because it is only temporary, a mother, despite fear or self-interest, must set no limits on the amount of this decision-making power which she will eventually hand over to her son. Consequently she sets no limits either on the extent to which she is prepared to trust him.

This feature of open-ended trust – this goal of total trust – is implicit, from the beginning, in the very nature of the parental relationship. And if a relationship of equality is to be eventually established, this trust must become explicit – usually through protest and disturbance of some kind. But if the intention and goal of total trust is denied in principle at any stage of the parental relationship, then the mother is implicitly denying the potentiality for maturity in her son. Hence she is also denying the very possibility of him ever having a relationship of equality with herself.

The Implications for the Clergy

The implications of this kind of total trust between clergy and laity, and the quality that would inevitably flow from it, are mind-boggling for a church which has until now structured its relationships along unequal hierarchial lines. It may be as well that the long-term implications of even small gestures of trust and empowerment are only gradually disclosed as the relationship evolves. However what has been done cannot be undone. The empowering process has been carefully set in motion. It has gathered momentum. Will it now be carried through to its logical conclusion by the laity? Will we find then that obsolescence is built into the very nature of the clerical/lay relationship too?

I am wondering then, what are the answers to certain key questions. Is clerical power merely a temporary power like parental power? If clergy do not accept in principle the idea of total trust of the laity, does this mean that the very possiblity of creating a relationship of equality – a community of equals – is being denied? And if this is so, does it mean that the teaching of Vatican II about the 'basic equality of all Christians' [5] is also being denied?

It is necessary that parental power – the mother's power to make decisions on her child's behalf – be totally let go, if she wants to bring about the full empowerment, maturity and equality of her son. Is this true of clerical power also? Does it too have to be totally let go in order to bring about the full empowerment maturity and equality of the laity? I invite you to ponder on my comparison and my questions, to read Vatican II and Pope John Paul II's statements about the equality and dignity of lay people, and if your answer to these questions is 'yes', then I invite you to work out the endless implications for yourself.

Notes

1. The analogy has limitations because I am not comparing like with like. In the clergy/laity relationship each group has both mature and immature members. Nevertheless the clergy as a group are powerful when compared to the laity as a group, in somewhat the same way as the mother is powerful in relation to the child.
2. I discuss a son rather than a daughter for the sake of clarity, as confusion can arise about pronouns when two people of the same sex are being discussed.
3. When a mother no longer plays an active role as teacher and protecter of her child, she has the freedom to create a new role, a new identity for herself. But this kind of freedom can be daunting for a mother who has not yet discovered her own strength and inner resources
4. When disturbance occurs in the parental relationship the mother is obliged to stand outside herself, as it were, in order to be her own questioner and critic. In the case of the clergy/lay relationship the more mature members of both groups can 'stand outside' the relationship and thus provide this necessary questioning and critique of the relationship.
5. There is need to explore further the phrase 'the basic equality of all Christians'. Such an exploration would have to address the question of the specific nature of the priestly ministry as distinct from the general priesthood of the laity. But such an exploration would require another article.

Inferiority or Good News?

Ned Crosby

The old celtic spirituality presents fantastic images of communion. God is all around like the air we breathe.

> There is no plant in the ground
> But it is full of His virtue
> There is no form in the strand
> But it is full of His blessing...
>
> There is no bird on the wing
> There is no star in the sky
> There is nothing beneath the sun
> But proclaims His goodness. (*Carmina Gadelica*)

Nobody is marginalised because God is with them. Nobody is inferior because the King of The Elements, God the Father, the Son and the Spirit are with us eternally:

> No anxiety can be ours:
> The God of the Elements
> The King of the Elements
> The Spirit of the Elements
> Close over us
> Ever eternally.

Such a wonderful vision and understanding of the incarnation! But, unfortunately, it was lost, way back in the *fadó*, and when we came along we did not expect to see angels on clouds, coming with peace and friendship to us. We were not born full of God's virtue, full of his blessing. We were born in sin. All our lives we were surrounded by the wickedness and snares of the devil. Satan, with his wicked wandering army, threatened our souls with ultimate ruin. In anxiety we lived, moved, and had our being. In fear and trembling we called on Michael the Archangel. God seemed faraway, forgetful, perhaps deaf. I cannot speak for all, but I certainly grew up in the middle of this vision: and always felt that my inferiority complex, Ballinrobe version, was part of the larger *Mayo, God help us* disease. Even now memory shakes out stories, anecdotes, experiences, and the virus of inferiority takes off again.

> As a child I was ashamed of Ballinrobe. My father was to blame. He came from Ballina. Ballina was bigger. It had the Moy and salmon. Rising in the Ox mountains it was a great 'swill' swaggering through Ballina, and hit the sea in style at Killala Bay. Poor Ballinrobe had only the Robe. After a slow start in a bog near Ballyhaunis, it snailed into the back of Ballinrobe gasping for breath.

Someone out of charity gave her a name. The Bulcan stream gave her the kiss of life below the bridge. She shuffled to a tired end, 'slithering' sideways into Lough Mask:
'Hardly a river at all', my father said, '... perch and a few starved pike.'
I used to sit on the bridge at Earls Mill and wish she was the Moy. But the Moy was far away.

Another story, carefully hoarded by inferiority in its complex, puts up its head:

Mary Maguire came out from confessions, wearing a yellow blouse, a green skirt and the highest heels we had ever seen. A different girl to the shy Mary who left for Boston three years before. We were 'the boys', gathered at the chapel railings for an eyeful. Imagine our surprise when she stopped. She spoke like a real Yank: 'Hi Boys', she said, as if she had a guitar in her nose, '... you guys should get the hell out of here; the system is wrong. It will never change.'
We jeered her back. Her parting words were a sting. 'Ah well, I guess you'll just stay forever stuck in the mud.'
She walked off like a film-star. Every swish of the green dress seemed to say she was above us, beyond us, miles too good for any of us, and the state we were in, down in a hole dug by the centuries. What was Mayo? What was Ballinrobe, on a darkish Saturday night at the Chapel railings, when compared to America, the beautiful! Mary, rechristened 'The Bombshell', left us in smithereens.

She was a glorious epiphany of a richer, brighter, faster life going on elsewhere, miles away. For us there was no glory, no riches and we were going nowhere. We were stuck in Mayo, worse still in Ballinrobe. Galway with its little University, and very conscious of its culture, still enjoys the odd chuckling *drochmheas* joke. Peel the joke and under its skin find the labels of inferiority and ignorance firmly glued to us.

J.G. McGarry being P.P. in Ballyhaunis, 'Gandhi', a homeless man, dies in Galway. The funeral goes to Ballyhaunis. The undertaker from Galway is impressed by the Mass, the music and the dignified send off. After the funeral the Canon thanks him. 'Not at all Canon. A lovely ceremony. It took me by surprise', to which the Canon replies, 'Thank God, we measure up to the Galway standard'.
Afterwards the undertaker adjourns to a pub in downtown Ballyhaunis for a jar or two of grief therapy. There he gleans the story of the Canon and brings it back to Galway with glosses.
'This Canon, ye see, came down from Maynooth and was all

about theology. Then he brought down these theologians to talk, but the people didn't turn up to hear them, d'ye see. They didn't want it. Why would they? Theology in Mayo? ' the undertaker added, 'for God's sake throw them a mangle and they'd ate it.'

A 'Nathaniel' remark, amounting to the old chestnut:
You can take the man from the bog
but you cannot take the bog from the man.

This sense of inferiority, the experience of being on the margin of life was aggravated and deepened by theology:

Across the Shannon, and past the bog of Allen stood Maynooth, the capital of the theological universe. Theology at Maynooth was the soundest and most pleasing to the Pope on the face of the globe. St Thomas sat on the theological throne. Aristotle, as I remember, was his batman, filling his inkwell, and putting 'snas' on his arguments. The 'good' life was manualised, moralised, legalised. Every moment of the day, from pyjamas back to pyjamas, was fixed. You always knew what you should be doing and where you should be. It was handing oneself over totally and tee-totally to your betters. It was hoping and praying to please and pass. It was avoiding such 'pitfallers' as squash in your closet or *Time* magazine under your mattress. Supernatural growth in grace, (the man on the throne not-withstanding) was based more on squelching and haltering the natural than on promoting it. So I understood and accepted myself as a slow bogwater river like the Robe. I had come for a change of water, hoping, like Ezechiel, to become a temple with four freshwater rivers flowing from my side. To a defeminised, delaicised, denaturalised compound, my inferiority complex, and I, had come to be washed, rinsed, ironed and starched into solid virtue. After seven years of long obeisance, punctuated by periodical judgement days at each of the seven steps, it was over. Now at last life was taking off. It was, in the clerical hierarchy:The cards were laid out on the table. God and his Bride, the Church, had been playing patience for almost two thousand years. Between them they slotted me in 'nicely' at the bottom, a humble ecclesiastical deuce. 'If you stick it out until your sacerdotage,' mused the diocesan wag, 'you'll finally come into your own.'

Another Way:

So much for the genesis of inferiority and the shaking up of memory. Just suppose I had been able to hear and understand something of the 'Good News'.

What would have happened I wonder, if I had always known

that The Robe was a sacred river? Would I have gone down the field at the back of our house and waited for the heavens to open? Would a 'voice' have told me I was a beloved Son? Would the Dove on the Barrack Wall have descended on me? Perhaps I should have remembered The Jordan, the local river of Jesus. There the Father spoke to him, there the Spirit came. He didn't spend time making derogatory comparisons with the Nile or the Blue Danube. The Jordan was not marginal or miserable. The Kingdom of God was there. There the declaration of the Father's love and delight were thundered into the ears of the world. It was around the Robe too, if only I had eyes to see and ears to hear. But somehow our small-town 'Hinduism' with its castes of village upperosity was central. I think I just assumed that our local hierarchy of worth, status, and dignity was laid down by God; was part of the order of nature; was so at the beginning and ever would be. It probably takes a long time for a colonised people to be liberated from the imperialism which opposed them. Seven heroic centuries, with uprisings in every generation may change the machinery of government. How long does it take to free the captive mind? How long to untie the complex of fear and inferiority and restore some native pride? Yet the Gospel offered such freedom and pride.

I should have reminded the undertaker (but I didn't) that Nazareth was not exactly a city of the tribes; that the angel of the Lord didn't seem to mind coming to a country girl in a village far away from the imperial city and the main highway; that 'marginalised' riff-raff were frequently the table companions of Jesus, and when Paul looked around him, as he spoke, he didn't notice too many top-brass, or *daoine galánta*.

Such Gospel moments however had little enough impact. God remained 'God' sitting in a 'Big House' transcendently perfect and powerful – an impossible Eileen Boyd.

> For months I would dawdle home
> At a respectful distance
> Behind the teacher's daughter
> Eileen Boyd, who lived
> In a house whose back garden
> Was visible from my window
> I watched her on summer evenings
> A white dress picking flowers
> Her slight graceful figure
> Luminous and remote
> We never exchanged greetings
> Her house was bigger than ours. (*Derek Mahon*)

The Big House theological mentality made easy approach to God so difficult. We became preoccupied with shaving off our natural beard and donning Sunday suits of piety and personality before we dared to knock at the holy door. Our minds, fueled by inferiority, magnified our local Big House mentality into cosmic proportions. We were preoccupied with what was great and what was little. Great Saints, great minds, great professors, and 'duds'. Unfortunately we left the healing words and stories sleeping in the scriptures.

The remarks of Jesus, recorded in the Gospels, about the hierarchies of his day are sharp. He advises his followers not to follow the example of those who sit in the chair of Moses; or model themselves on the lordly princes of the gentiles. Jesus was less than enthusiastic about people pushing themselves up front, putting titles before their names or letters after their names. The disciples asked the question: who is the greatest in the Kingdom of heaven? Jesus called a child and set her in front of them. The child is a subversive parable; explaining to the disciples and to us that all the dressed-up hullabaloo of hierarchy with its high-low, master-servant, boss-boy categories, have no place in the Christian community.

At the washing of the feet Jesus himself becomes parable. His dramatic gesture was like a time bomb planted in the expectation of the apostles. Peter's reaction, I think, represents a classical hierarchical imagination. Jesus had exploded his conventional Messiah with basin and towel.

Jesus had called his disciples to be 'with him'. He did not call them servants but friends. He did not overpower or dazzle. He was gentle and lowly of heart. Friendship happens when walls and hierarchy break down. Only when master-servant relationships are overcome can we meet in friendliness.

Ballinrobe knew its catechism. We had it on our tongues that the Incarnation was among the principal truths of our religion; but our hearts did not understand that, because of Jesus and the gift of that Holy Spirit, God was no longer remote but was 'with us'. We may have been too fascinated by a fear of hell, a success ethic, and Pelagian preaching. We continued to view the end of life as a degree day with Apostles, martyrs and medieval mystics in white gowns distributing scrolls to those who had made it. The chanting of the *Dies irae*, threatening calamity and misery was a mournful echo. The time of compassion had passed. God would be different now. Forgiveness and mercy would flicker out with our last breath, and the hearse would be driving us to judgment. Such horrific pedagogy cancelled the good news. Fear and inferiority went to town.

If only we had firmly believed that the end of life is communion: the table where north, south, east, west, blind, lame, deaf, poor and finally the rich will meet and eat, and where most of our categories of inferior-superior, crude-classy, success-failure, will come to their final end, and we will become a new creation.

If only we believed that the Eucharist was the sacrament of communion, microcosm of our cosmic end, an 'icon' in action of a final revelation and a glimpse into its nature! If we could have seen the Eucharist as God's oath that nothing, in life or death, could separate us from his life! If we knew it as a pledge of future glory – then perhaps we could have lived in joyful hope. How could we have understood then that the Father, Son and Holy Spirit lived in Ballinrobe, and not only in the Main Street chapel, but in every house and intimately in every heart? How do we understand it now? Wouldn't this be the important question?

Two Ways

The two ways continue: the way of inferiority and fear, and the way of good news and communion. Ballinrobe knows both ways.

A Ballinrobe man in a Galway hospital was told that his time was up. He asked, and the doctor told him he had less than a week to live. Fear and inferiority came to torment him, and guilt was with them. 'I was put into this world to know, love and serve God, and I have neither known, loved or served him ever. Now I'm terrified.' There were dreams: hawks hovering over his bed; black clouds ready to pour on him; a white coated figure with a microscope; a man raking up leaves under bare trees. 'I'm terrified of the judgement,' he said. Banquo's ghost stood invisibly by the bed, destroying remembered moments of achievement and celebration, shattering confidence. With him was Plato's Ghost, as ever, projecting the ideal-image he had not reached and now never would. Behind them stood his lifelong icon of 'God' as District Justice peering through the chronicle of his life, underlining his sins. If only Jesus could come and banish them. Fortunately he did come when a friend held his hand and told him the good news: that God's love was wild and passionate, that God had not been a stranger, that unknown to himself he had loved God when he had cherished his wife and held and hugged his children, because the two loves were now one; that indeed he had himself become the very compassion and largesse of God when he had received back his own prodigal son with ring and robe. 'I would be immensely comforted if I could believe that.' For two more days he struggled. On the third day the light came. It was the day of his Resurrection and his death.

Ballinrobe, I now realise, also knew the other way – the way of good news and communion. The old Celtic vision had survived in hidden places and lived its silent life. There was Paddy, who died one night last lambing season in the long field at Milehill:

> Real not notional
> wise and simple
> a man who did exist
> a man not just a dream
> no centre
> no margin
> instead communion
> lived for friends
> was friend
> lived for fields
> grew there
>
> Saw the immaculate conception
> of the leaves;
> Christ in the stable;
> seeds and slits of spuds:
> miracles
> each April
> in his fist;
> Redemption
> spread and stretched
> on a turf bank
> near Tuam;
> Larks were angels.
>
> Meals were holy;
> cap off for respect,
> face blessed
> for gratitude,
> card-table
> mass-table
> meeting-table
> Every table
> The Communion Table
>
> Died as you lived
> in the field
> helping a sheep
> 'one of the lambs was dead
> the other was saved'
> 'God be with you Paddy'
> as I pass the field

'Behold the lamb of God'
his spirit sings in the ditch

Paddy I hope the way
you were
Is coming tomorrow
for more.

Liturgy for Exiles

Thomas Waldron

A man and a woman are a natural enough starting point for any consideration of celebration, or faith, or liturgy. Any recipe – or receipt, I remember hearing it called oddly, and correctly, in Mayo as a child – begins properly with the ingredients, and a man and a woman are the proper and necessary ingredients for celebration, for faith, and for liturgy. Mixture, quantities, and treatment are variables, but in the biblical story the world begins with a man and a woman celebrating, and being celebrated. Adam delights in Eve. The first great Eureka of the human race is his cry, 'At last, here is one of my own kind.' And God who has 'grigged' him by showing him the animals first, must have said again, 'it is good,' – though that, and the laugh of delight that went with it, are not recorded. But then, as in all good liturgies, not everything should be spelled out. For liturgy is not rubrics, though the formal has its place.

Liturgy has to leave room for the wordless, for the joy or the sorrow or the thanks, or the delight, or the desperation that simply is and defies definition or description. Liturgy has to leave room too for the blanks that imagination and memory will fill, room for the winks of life, and for the smile and the nod and the understood that goes without saying. To put the millstone of a word round the neck of everything is to drown meaning.

So God and a man and a woman celebrated the world's first liturgy. They all celebrated creation, and they celebrated themselves and one another. God looked at Godself in the twin mirrors of man and woman, and he liked what he saw. God had said, 'And now we will make human beings and they will be like us and resemble us', and now looking at them, God was very pleased. And they walked with God, creatures and friends, united in the world's First Communion. They celebrated faith and hope and love, they celebrated relationship and meaning and mission. It was God who began liturgy and made what was needed for it – a world, a man and a woman.

'Take a man and a woman,' God said. So I'll take a Jewish man and a Mayo woman.

The Mayo woman told me she had been at Mass that Sunday. And I remembered that she had been at Mass on Saturday night. It puzzled me a little. 'I thought,' I said, 'you were at Mass yesterday.' (It is a part of a Mayo ritual, if not liturgy, to use 'I thought' even when you're certain – the definite can sound like an accusation, and people can have their own reasons). 'Well, I was,' she said, 'but the way it is, where Patrick is now, I don't think he can always get to Mass, so I go on a Sunday for him – in case he can't.' Patrick is her son. He's working in England, part of the great Mayo diaspora. That was the Mayo woman, saying no more than enough.

The Jewish man was Job. 'A sound man and a holy man,' the Jerusalem Bible calls him. And, as we know, he was a patient man. The bible tells us a little bit about him before his drama begins. 'Job's sons used to take turns giving a feast, to which all the others would come, and they always invited their three sisters to join them. The morning after each feast, Job would get up early and offer sacrifices for each of his children in order to purify them. He always did this because he thought that one of them might have sinned by insulting God unintentionally.'

That was the Jewish man, like the Mayo woman, saying no more than enough. 'In case he can't,' said she; 'unintentionally,' said he.

But both of them were sacrificing for their own, for the sake of the ones they loved, sacrificing instead of them and in case they wouldn't, or couldn't do it for themselves.

By its very origin, the word 'liturgy' celebrates interaction with and responsibility to and for the other. My picture of public work, which is what the word 'liturgy' means, belongs to an older Mayo. It's a picture of a *meitheal* of people gathered to save hay, people raking, turning, gathering, feeding forkfulls of hay to a man tramping, twisting of a rope, the arrival of tea and bread, the rest, the resumption. Creation was unified in moments like that – it ceased to groan, for it was saved. Man, woman, child, animal, growing things and tools, worked together in a field of salvation where everyone's work was valued. There was care for things – 'Be careful or you'll break the teeth in the good rake!' – and there was huge respect for the hay which in its new life would feed animals, who would feed people, and there was delight in the after grass which would be sweet and fattening for the cattle. And at the end of a summer's day, a woman would wander down simply to look at the field, green with golden dots, or a man would lean on a gate and his eyes would drink it in. As they looked, the unspoken word would be that of Genesis, 'it is good.' For liturgy is a world created, redeemed, proclaimed; it is Christmas, it is Easter, it is Pentecost.

After the fall, Adam is a diminished creature. His ease with God is gone and ease is a component of liturgy – that ease which is part of dignity, the ease that flows from a sense of one's meaning. Ultimately that meaning has its foundation in relationship, and the meaning is expressed most of all in mission. Some of the great figures of the Old Testament exemplify that ease, the meaning and the mission.

We find it in Abraham and the extraordinary dignity with which he proceeded in that testing which became a celebration of his faith. Abraham remains at his full height during all that story, conscious of meaning even when he cannot understand, conscious of mission even when he dreads it. Neither disaster nor triumph diminishes him. He moves and speaks calmly, invested as he is with faith in a God who loves him, and sure of the significance God has given him.

We find that same sense of mission and meaning in Moses. Moses is the meekest of men, 'the humblest man on earth' but he will assert himself before God. No one was more conscious of being mere man and no one is more conscious of the meaning conferred on him by his mission. He calls God to account, to maintain and to service his covenant of creation. He demands that God honour the image of himself and the mission of responsibility for the others given to himself, the man Moses.

So Moses plays the man. When God would punish Aaron and Miriam for their attempts to oust Moses, Moses cries out like a Redeemer, 'O God, heal her I beg you.' If God won't forgive his people then Moses asks, 'Blot me out from the book you have written.' His mission is salvation not destruction. He will not allow God to contradict his meaning.

This strength before God is the strength of faith. It moves in people who have heard God's word and taken him at his word. Neither Abraham nor Moses speaks as God's equal, but each speaks from a consideration of his own considerable meaning as God's image first of all, and God's agent secondly.

I don't think Job or the Mayo woman play or would see themselves as playing on the same stage as Moses, or Abraham. Job and the Mayo woman were redeeming their own small constituency. But – without speeches – they were equally sure that their constituency too was God-given and that they themselves were a God-send. In faith, in hope, in love, and in-stead, they make their sacrifice. They are sure of their God, sure of their relationship with God, sure of their own mission and meaning – and out of that certainty of faith they offer their liturgy of redemption. They are chosen to be, they choose to be, and they become, Redeemers.

'I know my redeemer lives,' said Job. It is part of the celebration of faith in liturgy that our Redeemers do live and that we are ourselves, Redeemers. We bring a lot of people to Mass with us and we ourselves are carried to God in arms at Baptism, but all our lives, on the prayers of fathers and mothers, husbands, wives and aunts and uncles and children, and people saying 'thanks' for us or saying 'sorry' for us to crying 'help' for us or simply sometimes in great love saying, 'Don't mind him, Lord. Take me. Let me stand for him.' – the very pattern of the ultimate Redeemer, Christ: 'Forgive them Father for they know not what they do. Greater love no man has than to lay down his life for his friend.'

For three years Christ's life was a liturgy. At Baptism, in the coming of the Spirit, in Communion of prayer, in the confession of those who came by night, in the forgiveness of sin, in his care for the sick, at a wedding in Cana, at a funeral in Naim, in constant ministry to the troubled, the bereaved, the bewildered, the desperate, in the companionship with the Twelve in the prelude to their priesthood, and on a Thursday and on a Friday, Christ celebrated liturgy of word and sacrament. He celebrated meaning and mission. He celebrated relationship. He walked and talked with God in gardens removed from Eden and mountains other than Sinai. He inserted himself into a world and into the lives of men and women around him. None was foreign. He celebrated faith wherever he found it.

All our liturgies are in the pattern of Christ's liturgy. They express his care, his regard, his respect, his responsibility for the other. They state and effect his intention of doing for the other what he or she cannot do for themselves. And their basis, and the final foundation of their power, is Christ's knowledge of and our faith in, the love and care of God for us. This Christ knew, this we believe. And our sacraments, our prayers, our pilgrimages, the Mass are statements of God's love and care. They symbolise the Genesis picture of God dreaming and delighted, seeing the possibilities of the human race and loving every minute and aeon of that vision, and the Genesis picture of man and woman praising God as they admired God's work – the world and each other. But that picture and relationship are not only symbolised in our liturgies. They are recreated and restored. The sacraments, the Mass don't just recall Eden, they recreate and restore it. That's why Job and the Mayo woman are the heart and soul of liturgy. With Christ they push open the gate that had clanged shut. They become with him the hand of God.

The Return from Exile

An English historian once saw God's presence in the world as like the hand of a parent on the saddle of a bicycle that a child was learning to ride. The child pedals and supplies the power, the child holds the handlebars and guides. The power comes unevenly, the guidance can be very erratic, but the hand on the saddle prevents collapse and catastrophe, and ensures ultimate triumphant arrival.

The sacraments are the reassuring presence, and the effective presence, of God in each one's personal journey. They celebrate our coming into the world, our coming to the table, the coming of personal responsibility, the beginning of adulthood, the choice of vocation, the care for the weakness of the body, and the daily life of the individual in the community, with all the responsibilities that being part of the Body of Christ entails.

So the sacraments reinforce the meaning of life. They challenge the temptation to say life is absurd. They are the evidence, the concrete signs of God's constant creation. He holds all things in being, but that holding is not indifferent or impersonal, and the sacraments are the signs of that. They are God's presence to the exiled spirit, – the light or cloud or star that accompanies the pilgrim on his way back to his homeland. The sacraments are Emmanuel – God with us.

And the Mayo spirit is always on the way home. We travel with our faces towards Mayo, whether we stand in woeful plight on the deck of Patrick Lynch's boat, or whether it's just a year ago today we left old Erin's isle. The celebration of the exile's longing and his return come naturally to us. Our songs match our sacraments. There is in both the songs and the sacraments the hope and the promise, of the eventual return. 'It's maybe some day I'll go back to Ireland, if it's only at the closing of my day.' The song may be a Galway song but it speaks for the Mayo of the spirit and that goes beyond Ballina to Belfast and Boston and beyond Castlebar to Cork and California. In our sense of exile the generality of Irish people are the same. When the sun goes down on *Galway Bay*, it's *Moonlight in Mayo* in a public house somewhere on earth. Like other exiles in another time, as they go through the Bitter Valley, in their hearts are the roads to Sion (Ps 83). And as we make our way to our homeland in heaven the sacraments are the attentions of our accompanying God.

All the sacraments celebrate the eventual return of the exile and the full restoration of prodigal sons and lost sheep and good thieves, and all those whose hands have been toughened by the thorns that grow West of Eden. They celebrate, too, reunion. Martha's arms go around Lazarus' neck, the widow in Naim weeps for joy, and a little girl skips to Jairus. All these fore-tastes of the paschal feast are proof positive that the promise of the sacraments will be fulfilled. And the sacraments promise restoration and reunion. The Mayo Association will one day have a full meeting and Christ will be the Mayo Person, not just of the year but of all time, and eternity. We celebrate our faith in that, as we celebrate every sacrament.

Every sacrament is a homecoming in miniature, in promise and in effect. It is incomplete but it is not ineffectual. Grace is glory in exile. The sacrament is not merely a sign of the return, it is a model of it, and it is part of it – it is the hand on the saddle preventing the fall, straightening the way. 'Rege quod est devium,' is the cry of the Pentecost sequence, 'Guide what's going astray.'

Baptism

Baptism is the bringing back into God's family of someone who walked out of Eden. It's the return of the Prodigal child and the father has open arms. 'Who have we here?' says God. 'This is Mary, this is Jennifer, this is Michael, this is Jonathan,' say the parents. 'Oh, come on in,' says God, 'Sure you're one of us. Pull in a chair, Jennifer. Make a bit of room for her there. Come in here near the fire, a ghrádh. It's awful cold outside.' Like father, God welcomes back Adam; like mother, God takes Eve's cold hands and warms them. The human being is at home again, in from the cold. Baptism is the sacrament of welcome, of *fáilte isteach nó arais*.

Confirmation

Confirmation began as a sacrament to bring people Christ loved back from the exile of fear. Fear had sealed the disciples in the upper room. The Spirit released them from the closed room and sent them out to bring Christ Risen to the crowds.

Shades of the prison house begin to close around the growing boy or girl. Wordsworth had it right. The loneliness of the intermediate position between child and adult is its own upper room. God struggles always to bring us out of ourselves, but he made a sacrament of his struggle for the adolescent. With chrism and the hand of the successor of those first confirmed, the apostles, he invites boy and girl into the adult world, and says again, 'Courage, all you people of the country! – it is the Lord who speaks. To work! I am with you – it is the Lord of Sabaoth who speaks – and my spirit remains among you. Do not be afraid!' (Hag 2:4-5)

Penance

Sin is exile. It is originally exile from Eden and from communion with God. It is classically participation in the exile of Cain, sent away from the community of people, for all sin is Cain's sin – betrayal of relationshhip with God or brother. It is energy gone wrong – a black hole created by the implosion of the spirit. Penance has always been seen as return, the road back to God and community. Christ provided the sacrament of penance as a vehicle of return. But that is to state it drably, and to miss part of its celebration.

Christ painted penance with two faces – the face of a woman laughing with delight, the face of a man striding home, strong and happy. Both had found something they had lost and both called for others, a commmunity, to join them in joy. You can sin on your own. You cannot celebrate on your own. And, says Christ, God doesn't celebrate alone either. But Christ doesn't just make Penance the picture of happiness – he puts sound with picture. It's the sound of angels cheering.

Ordination

It might seem that ordination has little to do with exile. But a priest is simply a function of exile. Only a people in exile need priests. In heaven there will be no shortage of priests, because none will be needed there. The gathered harvest needs no labourers.

And the celebration that commonly attends the ordination of a priest is the celebration of a people gathered round a campfire. A pilgrim people naturally travelling in a line, related in linear fashion, stops and gathers itself in a circle round one person. They gather in imitation of the final gathering, and in expectation of it. They gather in celebration of someone among them who is a promise of the last home-coming, and a sign of God's presence and his care for his people. In the more sober liturgy of ordination, the people have called for and accepted this person. Through years of faith and prayer they have produced him. Now with music and singing and dancing and flags and feasting, they celebrate themselves and their hope, and him and their faith in him. To-morrow the caravan will move on, but to-night it is stopped.

And the celebration honours every kind of relationship, special honour to the nearest, but a place for the most distant cousin, for the oldest in-law, for the fellows who went to school with him, and the girls who might have married him, his first teachers, his latest professors, and a man from India that he met in London when he worked there as a deacon. All are gathered and, all are one in their focus and their loyalties and their wishes. It is in its unity, its theme, and its celebration, a foreshadowing of Christ drinking the wine now with his disciples in the achieved kingdom. But in itself it is a celebration of faith.

Alleluia
'God has given us another Christ'
Alleluia
'Someone whose coat tails we can cling to'
Alleluia,
Procedamus.

(And, please Lord, don't let him forget that it was you and we who gave him the coat!)

Marriage

Even in Eden there was a sense of loneliness. We don't realise that until we hear Adam's delight in Eve. 'At last!' – it is a man's cry as he rounds the last corner of a long journey and sees home. And the loneliness of the psyche can be a very long journey indeed. Even God was not quite enough to still that sense of psychic exile in Adam. As God created him there was need for another. In heaven

God will be all in all, but on earth, Eden or outside – man and woman need each other. So God made the sacrament of marriage.

Everywhere on earth the sacrament is celebrated, in shadow and in substance. Everywhere on earth, whatever its local rules, it is celebrated as the ordinary answer to the human cry for a personal pleroma – the fullness that the incomplete being searches for always. I have read that the crowning of the bride and groom as King and Queen in the Greek Church is done as a sign that, for those two human beings on this happy day, the prayer 'thy kingdom come' is achieved – for this day anyway.

Even the failures, those who fail because they are incapable of the intimacy they long for, those who fail to find anyone, those who fail to find the right one, all the botched and repeated attempts of marriage are tragic evidence of the exiled spirit seeking someone with whom it can find home and rest. An Intermediate Certificate boy once wrote for me how frustrated he was that he could only partially reveal himself even to his best friends, but that 'someday, somewhere I hope to meet someone to whom I can tell everything.' I think Adam would have understood his cry.

And so would the young Mayo man who found the girl to whom he could tell everything. She died, a young wife and mother. He says that now as he hears Mass the words that mean most to him are the words of the prayer after the Our Father, 'Protect us from all anxiety, as we wait in joyful hope for the coming of our Saviour, Jesus Christ.' He looks forward to that day when he will meet her again, with Christ – just as on the day he married her. And he'll tell her everything.

Marriage is the meeting of exiles who create home. So all who have known the pain of exile celebrate home as they find it at a wedding. We warm our hands at a new fire cast upon the earth, and pray for young hearts and the new hearth. At that moment, we are like God in Genesis, like him in thanksgiving, and like him in trepidation. For we know not only the desires of the exile, but also the demands of exile, and we pray and hope that a man and woman will be able, will get the grace, to answer both. We celebrate, conscious that here be serpents.

The Sacrament of the Sick
A priest told me about celebrating the sacrament of the sick with a family. They were gathered round their father, and he said the prayers, first the generic prayer which says, quoting Saint James, that the priest should be sent for, and that the prayer of faith will save the sick person. There followed the personal prayer for this man John, a father, very ill, very much loved, now in exile from the mobile healthy busy community. Then the priest, as the Ritual says, laid his hand on the sick man, and so did the man's family, wife,

sons, daughters. And the priest saw the hands as a strong prayer to God, to draw back to their daily community their exiled father and a strong statement to their father of their love for him. There they were, like Christ – imposing hands in love, the outstretched hand, Christ's strongest prayer, drawing back to health if they could, but in any case, imploring God for his help. And in community with God their love was cancelling the exile. Love is stronger than any of our deaths.

Often in someone else's illness we find ourselves dumb and helpless. In the sacrament of the sick, our faith finds a way to say and our love finds a way to do. Then with the oil of healing and word of comfort, Christ assures and reassures. And we are all those people he ever turned to, centurion and servant, father and demented son, woman who had gone to every doctor, Peter and Peter's wife and Peter's mother-in-law. His long shadow falls on those who suffer and those who love them, and we celebrate his presence in the sacrament which says, 'I'm here and I know.' We celebrate the solidarity of Christ on the day we need him. For the sacrament of the sick is not your everyday sacrament – but it is the sacrament for some day. The day comes for us all when someone says, 'I think he'd like to see the priest.' It's the courteously tentative, graciously conditional way of asking for what we are absolutely sure is there – the help of Christ.

Eucharist

The story goes that a crowd of Aughamore men – Aughamore, Mayo that is – were rampaging in a pub in Manchester, taking it over. In the middle of the mayhem, a black man was seen standing on a table waving the leg of a chair and shouting, 'Me an Aughamore man too!'

Both as individual and communities we are always in danger of collapsing inwards. Simply said, we find it easy to be selfish, singly or in groups, family, profession, union, country. The Methodist Bedside Book quotes an 18th century jingle:

> We are the sweet selected few
> The rest of you be damned
> There's room enough in hell for you
> We won't have heaven crammed.

The lines belong to all people in all centuries!

Christ instituted the eucharist to defeat this inward collapse. It is the eucharist which lights up the paradox of exile – that as we exile others, we ourselves become exile, indeed are more deeply exiled. Christ, the eucharist, is against all our exclusions and exclusivities. And, of course, it is significant that Saint John puts the washing of the feet into his story, instead of, and where we would expect to find, the institution of the eucharist. When Peter protests about the meniality of Christ the Servant washing the feet of Peter the pontiff, Christ tells him, 'unless I wash your feet you shall have no part with me.' We have to be both washers and washed.

A Mayoman in New York once told me that the way to get on in New York was to remember that, 'one hand washes the other and both hands wash the face.' It is a proverb coined by the children of this world, but it perhaps states the truth of what Christ tried to teach the children of light – we are all the great unwashed – to use the phrase of Edmund Burke, whose ancestors no doubt like those of a lot of Mayo people, once set out in a boat from Normandy.

So the gathering round Christ, Sunday after Sunday, to break the bread and tell the story, is a gathering to state and to symbolise the truth that we are all God's children.

Psalm 86 says, 'In you all find their home.' That Aughamore man who stood on the table in Manchester (or wherever he stood on it – the authors differ – and it makes no difference, it only adds to the truth of it), that black Aughamore man had it right. Colour or country or creed, he was an Aughamore man. It is one of the fundamental truths that we state and celebrate in the eucharist. By his incarnation, Christ became an Aughamore man too. We are all Aughamore men. Christ says he cannot rest until that theoretical truth becomes actual truth. And if we are all Aughamore, then, by definition, we are all Mayo. So welcome in – and isn't that where we began in Baptism? And isn't that where we will end in heaven? In the meantime, we go to Mass.

Funerals

Tom used to say, 'There won't be many at my funeral. But sure there were only six at Jesus Christ's and look where he got.' In fact that church was full for Tom's funeral, and nobody was surprised because he was a great one for going to funerals himself.

The funeral is one of the great Christian liturgies and it has always celebrated our faith, our hope and our love. It has always been, in rural Ireland, one of the great gatherings and the great epiphany of kindness and sympathy and reconciliation. Fading friendships are renewed, blood relationships are reasserted, marriage relationship is honoured. Even neighbours who might bicker or be jealous or cool or not talking – their hardness melts in the presence of death, and they come to help, the women with tea and cakes and apple tarts, the men with company and reminiscence. Friends come, of course, but 'the friends' come and have a special place – these are people who might or might not be distant cousins but, who are closer friends than nearer relations. 'The connections' will be there too – not quite in-laws but the people related in the complexity of the marriages of cousins and uncles and aunts. There will be people there to reciprocate attendance because 'they were always at our funerals.' Reciprocity has some claims to be a gospel virtue, 'forgive us ... as we forgive.' 'In the measure you give, it shall be measured to you.'

The dead person's first gift is in the pattern of Christ's – a communion of people, a sign of peace, the grace of kindness, the incense of charitable words, the creation of goodness. The second century pagans were astonished that second century Christians went singing from church to grave – 'they escort the body with sounds and thanksgiving as if the dead person were setting out from one place to another nearby.'

They would still be astonished in Mayo to-day. The Christians still come to escort the body. It matters very much to them that they should be there. They feel the letter of sympathy or the Mass Card on its own is a lesser tribute which must be excused. But in person or by letter or by card, they will pray that the journey to heaven will be a short one. They know where Jesus Christ got to, and they'll wish their dead friend right beside him – *ar dheis Dé.*

Conclusion

Liturgy is the work of the crowd, but not the work of a drifting crowd. It is not the work of the crowd that looks like sheep without a shepherd. There is a shepherd and the shepherd is Our Lord. With him we shape our liturgies, sacraments, sacrifices and prayers. Liturgy gives us our bearing on our journey in time. It gives us fixed points to which to relate the moments of our lives and the movements of our progress.

By baptism we belong, penance is an anchor, communion is a promise. Liturgy breaks the link between yesterday's guilt and today's work, and tomorrow's anxiety. Time and the business of time tends to dissipate faith because in the business of time, we produce so much that can become false gods. Our liturgies contradict our deifications. Liturgy condenses and concentrates the relation of people to God. Our faith is celebrated at its most intense when in liturgy we pray with others, when in liturgy we pray for others and become, in our own small and marvellous way, redeemers, images of God and vicars of Christ. It's a high vocation for Mayo and for all, God help us. But we come of very good stock. The mother and father were great friends of God's. Well, there was a falling out all right, a bit of coolness. But we fixed it up with the Son. Things are all right again – the finest.

PART III
Atlantic God

Journey from Achill
John Deane

An abiding memory of Achill Island: long before dawn, at the crossroads in Bunnacurry, family groups gathered to put an emigrating son, brother, or father, on the early bus to Westport; there were cases, trunks, bags and a restrained murmuring of voices; I do not remember any sort of wailing, only that sense of a density of suffering consistent with helplessness, with the bleakness of rain, with the all-embracing demands of a faith that was negative in its impulses; we cry, poor banished children of Eve, mourning and weeping, embracing our sufferings until we are spirited through to the great hereafter.

Island Woman
It wasn't just the building of a bridge,
for even before they had gone by sea
to Westport and from there abroad, and each
child sent money home till death in the family
brought him, reluctant, back. Of course the island
grew rich and hard, looked, they say, like Cleveland.

On a bridge the traffic moves both ways.
My own sons went and came, their sons, and theirs;
each time, in the empty dawn, I used to pray
and I still do, for mothers. I was there
when the last great eagle fell in a ditch.
My breasts are warts. I never crossed the bridge.

Our Roman Catholic faith was persistent as Achill rain, associated with physical and spiritual endurance, and vaunted as the force which maintained Ireland strong down the centuries in spite of persecution, famine, and deportation. As a child I was bathed in all of that, and the insidious power of aloofness and of dogged determination held me back a little way from life.

Mother
God, on our island, insinuated himself –
like the thousand varieties of rain –
everywhere; soundless, shifting,

sometimes a brute and wailing
battering against our homes, a memory –
in our lives' dark outhouses –

of famine-gnawed, bitter people
herded onto piers.
Faith of our fathers, mother sang,
in spite of dungeon, fire and sword.

Her kingdom the resinous loft, school
girls about her, their hair, their smell,
how they huddled together derisively;

the priest, on the tiny altar,
took his cue from her,
breathless harmonium, diapason, celeste.

By the pamphlet rack,
by the window ledge
where the unclaimed glove,

the beads, the sacred medal, lay with a few
dead and dying flies,
a darkwood staircase led

to mystical heights.

*

A vision before her of something perfect
she corrected us, ticking us off; be
true, she would say, be true of her

till death; she would sit with exercise books,
crossing the 't's, insistent, deft;
cancer spread in her and her body shrank,

blemishes, like ink-blots, on wrist and face;
her mind careened, ungovernable. She sat
high in her hospital bed, absorbed,

corrected hand-writing on her get-well cards.
When she died there were beads
under the pillow, nest-coiled, a lip-stained cross,
the rosary bird, brooding.

Inevitably, in the mind of a child, the images and the thrust of such a faith run deep. And all was by no means negative; the deeply universal beauty of much of the rituals, and experiences of such an upbringing, do leave a sense of some truth, some mystery and some beauty that will not be shaken off in a lifetime. In Bunnacurry, Achill Island, there was a monastery of the Third Order of Saint Francis; they had a boy's national school attached, where I was taught by the brothers. And we went to Mass in the monastery chapel, perhaps during the seasons of Lent and Advent, perhaps on special feast days; I know it was always early in the morning, and I drowsed; but I did experience a glow of some safe and warm surety, the brothers on their predieus beyond the special rail that kept the tiny public back, the shuffling, the immediacy and accuracy of the Latin responses, the heads bowed for communion, the brother at the door smiling at us, and we knew we would meet him again later on that day, in the school.

The Monastery

On Achill Island it has been another tart summer;
the monastery gate has rusted closed
and monastery buildings crumble;

only the cemetery flourishes, Leo, Rufus, Anthony...
The chapel floor is rotting wood;
at dawn a pale blue ghost will cross

slowly, shivering. I keep a shard
of cobalt-blue glass upon a shelf,
savouring its light, its patterning.

*

with its sheds and orchards
an island upon an island;
I was white dough then in many hands;

we drove in the warmth of half sleep to Mass,
the slow, sedate black Anglia
parked on gravel where yellow light

reached from the chapel door;
we entered; in overhanging branches
rooks began to grumble.

*

Plaster saints
with plaster lilies in their hands
looked down on polished floors;

Angelo's head was straw;
his sandals slubbered on the chapel floor;
it was he who brought the candleflame

up from the cells to the honey, altar, light;
the flame grew large and welcoming
behind the cobalt-blue glass of the door.

The brown coiffed figures on their predieus
were ranks of worker angels;
Angelo's head was straw; I heard him snore

and his head would loll
as if Botticelli's messenger forgot,
for a moment, his awful declaration.

*

Brother Leo's one glass eye
could penetrate all wickedness
behind the lavatory walls;

his good eye watched you
watching the fixed stare of the other.

There were brass sliding trapdoors
over inkwells on the desks; 'dip' he would say
'your filthy fingernails down deep
and write the purity of God into your skulls.'

Those who forgot their Bible History
were made to chew on sour apples;
'the taste' he would say 'of sin is bitterness'.

*

Juniper's rhubarb pie
was two feet long, two inches wide;
'twon't take me long' he'd say 'to wait

a lifetime for my God.' Juniper
has been in the slaughter-house again, begging;
he will make such trotter soup,

such succulent stews that the poor
will rise from their beds and cry out to the Lord
oh Juniper, oh brother, Brother Juniper.

Juniper has cut
cloths from his cowl and habit;
he has shared out altar tapestries

and made vests for the labouring fishermen;
away on the road the tankers
ferry shark oil, shark blubber,

and the air thickens with the stench;
sometimes the hillside furze are molten gold
and rhododendron woods at Achill Sound

play hautboy processional music;
Juniper's pockets were deep, with traces of God
among mints, liquorice, and ticks of dust.

Even then, although this may be a wilful interpretation with the benefit of hindsight, I think I sensed some unease at this faith; there were the people of Achill, dressing up for Sunday Mass, many of them standing about outside the church until Mass was over, all of them seemingly given over to their faith; and yet the whole panoply of Roman Catholicism seemed to have nothing to do with their sufferings, the emigration, the dole, their heaving of nets from curraghs, their scraping away at sandy soil, their digging through the bogs for fuel. Only those silly-seeming brothers who came out and walked and worked among the people, seemed to me to have something more real about them. And my love for

Francis of Assisi must go very much deeper than the magic of his myths, or the reality of his presence among us even today.

To jump away a little, the sixties in Ireland stand out for me as the end of the Middle Ages. Suddenly, entirely new perspectives seemed to be opened up on every aspect of living. Challenges were put to every lane and alleyway of our faith and for me the challenges proved too great: the faith had no response, and I lost my faith. Perhaps my own awareness of the great world outside the island of Achill, and outside the island of Ireland, grew as the awareness of our century began to grow; Vietnam, the horrors of South Africa, the terrible struggles of the peoples of Latin America, the plight of the poor in Ireland, as the whole thrust of our own country seemed to turn in favour of the rich and the newly rich. And everywhere I heard the answer of the church and it was 'No! No! No!' to any possibility of change and growth. Faith was simply left behind; it was irrelevant; it even became an affront to people trying to come to terms with our times.

Faith, in me, had dwindled to a sentiment, an uneasiness; and yet I continue to believe that there is more for mankind than this mere trafficking in goods, in pleasure, in the lives of others. The sense of a search has kept me restless. It was in reading Eberhard Bethge's life of Dietrich Bonhoeffer that I began to get a vague notion that Christ ought to be brought in from the cold of Catholic dogma, and made to permeate the whole of life. It was, if I understand it rightly (and I am no theologian, no scholar) a new 'worldly interpretation' of Christ that could enrich our language, and hence our lives. I dread the jargon of politics, and of church politics; and I responded to Bonhoeffer, with a sense of excitement, as of something rich, but undeveloped. Is it a totally ludicrous hope that Christ-ness could pervade the language first and then the deeds of our men-in-charge? Or will we see the untruth of political jargon lead again and again towards a holocaust?

In the Custody of the State

They came, those days, in Ford and Austin,
stood outside the Chapel on the boundary wall;
words they used, gesticulating words;

sometimes the men threw hats into the air
that fell again, like shot pheasants.
They appeared, a while, on days

given over to the dead when we walked,
hands crossed awkwardly over the crotch,
the long walk to the yew field;

    on Sundays, after prayers, we tensed
to the disembowelling of the hare and went home,
spent, after the masturbation. Bonhoeffer

had hoped that Christ the Leader
would conspire in the attempt on Hitler's life;
he heard someone crying loudly in the next cell,

words would not reach,
he banged on the wall between.
In Buchenwald, we were told,

a man held up his hands before his face,
saw them melt down to the bone in flames. But we,
they told us, know enough of wars

never to be surprised again.
Today they come, in Saab and Peugeot,
cruise our streets with loud, recorded, words;

should you suggest – Christ –
as working hypothesis in Party, Senate, Dail,
they will laugh, and cough, and sicken.

Bonhoeffer walked out calmly to the scaffold;
he climbed the wooden steps towards the omega;
brave and composed he stepped out onto darkness;

we are crying out against a great, blank, wall.

From the encounter with Bonhoeffer it was an easy progression to the discovery of 'liberation theology'. I think the negative response of Pope John Paul II to the liberation movement in Nicaragua helped to focus my attention on what was happening in Latin America. Leonardo Boff was also introduced into my awareness by being summoned to explain himself before the same gentleman. From Rome again it has been 'No! No! No!' (a form of 'Out! Out! Out!', an attitude that has given another word to our language, Thatcherism). But Boff's message, and that of Gustavo Gutierrez, excites me greatly, and from it I see the hope for our world, and my personal path towards understanding.

    This is talking 'revolution', but revolution in the sense of revolving, of going back yet again to the source, to the living, working Jesus. It is talking 'revolution' in the sense of turning, of repenting, of changing one's ways; our 'cultural ethos is being invaded destructively by the myth of progress in the capitalist mold and its attendant focus on high consumption by small elites' – Boff; here we must repent, we must turn back, unlike the sufferer of Eliot's 'Ash-Wednesday, 1930':

JOURNEY FROM ACHILL 141

> Because I do not hope to turn again
> Because I do not hope
> Because I do not hope to turn...

And it is talking 'revolution' in the sense that it seems to be happening in East Germany, that we had hoped, for a short and heartwarming summer, was happening in China, bloodless, people-inspired, inevitable, and true. In Achill Island there was a young man named Thomas Patten, born 1910, who became unhappy with his people's lot and worked to better it; this meant emigration to begin with, but his heart was fired with the same love of the people that led so many to Spain in 1936 to take up arms against the same sort of fascism that is more quietly rampant in our times. His story tells of revolution, of violent battle and its pointlessness, and the way life goes on, the heavy, turning wheel of time. There is a stone erected in Dooega, Achill, on which is written: 'Thomas Patten, Achill, 1910-1936 who fought bravely and died in the defence of Madrid, 1936, for the Spanish Republic and for all oppressed people'.

Revolution

Born among these beautiful, tedious mountains,
these lazy-beds; names about him:
Inishgalloon, Gubglass, Loughanascaddy;

sea-kelp scattered on the fields;
beyond – the Atlantic, world movements;
night sky above the village
an armada of possibilities.

He would spread his rug out on Dooega Strand,
days when his father would still swim
and Grannie, leaning her back against the rocks,
loosened the blouse above her wholesome breasts;
he held the cranefly, daddy-long-legs, in his fist,
knew its scrabbling helplessness;

impatient he hurled rocks into the sea.

Kilburn, 'The Red Lion', where he paused
from his building of the city to be best man;
he wears a suit, a tie, a white carnation
and gazes out, with candour, on the future.

Then there were other names to deal with:
Guernica, Pamplona, Cordoba,
the dark bull of the people humbled in the ring
while the general, smiling, was having his portrait done;
death, the harvestman, tightening its limbs about him.

Dusk, Dooega Bay; a stone
set among heathers carries Patten's name;
he is watching out over the bay towards the stars;
a curragh has scraped home against the pier;
there are words, laughter, the echo of wood on wood;
to-morrow they will scatter dried sea-kelp over the fields.

The face of Thomas Patten gazing out from the stone over the ocean is a strong reminder of the ongoing suffering of the people, and of the indomitable will to better the people's lot. But in all of this our 'faith' still seems irrelevant: until the realisation comes that the 'faith' we were hustled into is a divergence from the truth of Christ. The kingdom of God, as Boff points out, is already with us, its physical manifestation depends on the achievement of a total 'liberation' of all peoples from the shackles of poverty, exploitation, domination, and every move we make that enables this liberation to be developed more fully is a truly Christ-ian act. The most meaningful phrases I have encountered in decades comes again from Leonardo Boff: 'The christic structure is anterior to the historical Jesus of Nazareth. It pre-exists within the history of humanity. Every time a human being opens to God and the other, wherever true love exists and egoism is surpassed, when human beings seek justice, reconciliation and forgiveness, there we have true Christianity and the christic structure emerges within human history... With Jesus Christ Christianity received its name. Jesus Christ lived it so profoundly and absolutely that his surname became Christ.' (from *Jesus Christ Liberator*, Leonardo Boff, SPCK 1980)

At last, in the writings and in the example of priests working in Latin America, I came to believe again in the possibility of Utopia. Here is an agenda, a Christian agenda, that gives thrust and meaning and hope to our activities. Francis of Assisi again becomes the great exemplar; or even someone as tortured and as true as Vincent Van Gogh; and suddenly a Dublin supermarket with its glut of supplies becomes the occasion for the theology of liberation:

Delikat-Essen

At the far right of the superstore
the meats garden – discreet lighting,
hallucinatory waterfalls;
only progressive democrats shop here,
feeding off lives
crushed under the belly of history;

neat rows of quail, all trussed and dainty
like young girls' breasts;
rabbits, hares, caught in flight and skinned,
laid out nude, purpling, like babies;

chops, here, have been dressed in frilly socks;
on trays, as if a Salomé had passed,

are livers, kidneys, hearts, and tongues.
Among these classically landscaped meatbeds –
low hedges of parsley sprigs,
cress, sculpted tomato busts –
you will find the names absent from history.
Oh to stand on a wooden Chiquita banana box

and urge theologies of liberation!
but all who come
nod to the government officials in their white coats,
machetes, bone-saws in their holsters,
and blood - like maps of Uruguay, Guatemala and Peru -
staining their elegant tuxedoes.

Against the awful and ongoing violence that seems endemic to our times, liberation theology can set up an example of Christ-ness; for me Gorbachev is a saint in this category, and those with power who continue to exploit that power for the mere economic aggrandisement of their already wealthy class, become the great figures of evil of our time. The terrible tragedies brought about by the violence of certain factions in the North of Ireland occasionally throw up an irony that leads to the imposition of some liberation contrasts – as for instance the placing of a ransom demand of unusual gruesomeness behind the statue of St Theresa of Lisieux, perhaps the most gentle of our heroines, and the most free under the terms of her own, deliberate, bonding.

Remembrance Day
Behind the statue of St Teresa of the Flowers
a brown package, the message, the ransom note.
Somewhere a room where men in balaclavas

play at dice; safe houses. Rose petals
fall on us from the clouds. A soldier
brooks over the named and the unnamed dead

of another war; the cenotaph; the empty tomb.
The gable end of a street
has swollen out like a balloon; our prayers

are pinned like poppies into our lapels.
Our arms have been growing into wreathes.
In the quiet of the night we go on crying, very hard.
*

After the bombardment apple-blossom fell
like snow in Normandy; retreating soldiers pushed
through Caen towards Paris. Under rubble of her town

a little saint lay undisturbed; I choose,
she had said, everything, her arms folded,
her eyes held down, turning and turning

in the chestnut-tree walk of her convent grounds,
the sky above her full of leaves, like prayers;
someone comes, with wheelbarrow and rake, and works

among the shadows of the trees. When they clothed her
snow fell on her garden, and the chestnut-trees
were apple orchards blossoming.

Is it totally naïve to hope that the utopia discoverable in the surge towards liberation emanating from the peoples of Latin America and elsewhere may yet bring about a radical alternative to the greed and slavery of the west? Is there even the remotest possibility that the general sense of distrust in our political leaders and their words may uncover some with the original christic sense of truth about them? My own journey, pilgrimage, voyage, or circling, began in Achill Island and has moved far afield in its urgency and its quest. And I do feel that if a faith as deeply felt as the one I was brought up to is ever to emerge, then it must be one that answers all the physical and spiritual demands of a living, toiling people. Our century is drawing to a close; it has been one of wars and pollution, of incalculable oppression, of military inventiveness that is truly diabolical; how will our times be remembered? It is doubtful if a great deal of love will be evident from our century. In Achill Island there was a person who suffered greatly, because of war and the callings of war, yet who exhibited in her life the great patience and impulse towards love that will make her memory rich and warm in my mind. It is that same sense of home, of generosity, of innate and unspoilt kindness, that I continue to associate with the island of Achill, west of Europe, west of Ireland, across that little space of Atlantic ocean, where I was born and where my spirit still finds sanctuary.

Nora

Her bramble fingers clutch the eiderdown;
the bedroom hers again, no man, no child
intruding; the muscular, dark wardrobe
has long been emptied of the master's smell;

now the century is dying as she dies,
its individual numbered years becoming history;
her name floats free of her, towards memory,
the last decade – she will not see it out;

there ought to be no killing-places here,
no residues of war, yet this gross century

inveigled even her sons from her. I watched her,
vulnerable at her prayers, as Christ was;

I, being the youngest, led the final
decade, and then we prayed silently a while,
the kitchen clock presiding, turf settling
in the grate; the tutts and sissings of her prayers

called out beyond the emptiness. Someone
will come, with fingertips draw down her eyelids,
close the gaping mouth. I will remember
being gathered in her love, I will say her name

Nora, Nora, to the emptiness. On the far side
of the century who will remember
our suffering? Will they name our times with a shudder?
barbarian decades, grasping metallic years.

Cassandra Island in Mayo
Patrick O Brien

On an uninhabited island off the Mayo coast there is an image of the crucified Christ. To encounter it, to meet it in its raw but embalming simplicity, it is necessary to arrive on Caher Island by small currach in a time of peace. Wind, storm, turbulent sea prevent passage. Then, once in a while, the weather opens up to landing. It is a daunting place. From the refuge of the mainland it has the uncanny look of a whale at rest. As if it has just released some Jonah on a reluctant shore.

This biblical imagery takes on resonances as you explore the island interior. For deep in its belly there is a remnant of God's call. The skeleton of this hope are the bare bones of the earliest days of Christianity in Ireland now sinewed with moss and lichen. At its breastplate there is a church, its altar opened to the moods of the western sky. Beside it, a rough stone-walled structure known as the Saint's Bed. To this come a shuffling pilgrimage of the sick, invited by legend and faith to know a healing of mind and body. Indeed the whole island is venerated by nearby island fishermen. Sails are dipped in passing, hats removed in obeisance to the sacred. Around the church, protecting it in a rib cage of caring, are a stations of the cross — a series of carved images on limestone. The anonymous monk sculptors brought a depth, feeling and skill to bear on the stone. The lethal simplicity of the cross is led slowly to life. The stark straight lines of death are flooded with circles. A faint heartbeat. A sun rising in morning mist. Here and there the lines reach out to touch new shapes, to explore the stones' own life and strength. On one station two dolphins beat their way under the tide of falling blood. They seem to promise guidance to a welcoming haven. All of these, might, indeed would, have their interest as relics of a lost time. Of concern only to archeologists. But one image rescues Caher Island, gathers it into the present moment and looks uneasily towards the future. One cross, on a slight promontory, a small Calvary, bears one of the earliest images of Christ's face.

Centuries of barbed wind, of neglect and loss have dulled the sculptor's hand until now the face barely distinguishes itself from the stone of its creation and death. It is closer to skull than face, its flesh a victim of time. Green lichen suggest another life, however, regained in the depths of the earth and the face's humility before grass seems to gather all to itself. The stone and stars, the squall of sea birds, the lowing call of seals, the remorseless millennia, the pain and joy of our presence. To stand, kneel before it, touch it, riskily, with the eyes of fingers, to pray its peace, is to enter its echoing spirit. You hear words uttering their new shapes. There is certainly the morning dew freshness of the gospel on these harsh shores. A place where memory stutters of beginnings: genesis words. But equally there are cries of abandonment. For Caher Island, as a living community, ended with the invasion of the warrior Vikings, the long ships of sword and rapacity. And today a dark cloud over the ruins and tombs recalls the funeral processions of Northern Ireland and El Salvador. The wind and cruel years, the unpeopled place, speaks also of a threatened future. Of a country laid bare by uncaring economics, of lands devastated by empires and religious identities and feuds. Of an earth itself blasted by nuclear warfare and war preparation. Of an island planet shivering in the black sea of ecological poison. We kneel here today painfully aware of the frailty before the earth's future. Before war and hunger, before the hatred and dark violence against women and minorities. We kneel broken and meet the face of Christ. The face that bears the mark of Cain, the blood and tears of the victims. That limped, lucid face looks into our eyes, looks through their tears and flesh with a patient memory and invitation. Of dark hours dawned to light; of tombed hopes wombed to life.

In the survival of this icon we have deep clues to the survival of the human face. Part of the clue lies in its isolation. The monk sculptors chose the island loneliness, a place at several removes from the centres of power. Their life here, their prayers, their art and community lay like a questionmark outside the mainland of society and thought. Their crucified Christ attests to this. For this Christ was, is, an abandoned figure. Religious power and the taloned eagle of Rome, preying strength, have conspired to this bloody end. Friends (except for a few, a mother, a lost prostitute, the faithful friend, John and one or two waifs along the sorrowful road – Veronica's towel holding the image of truth's blood, Simon hefting the burden of others) have departed for safer shores. Yet out of this crucifixion of hope, in a way known only to God beyond the strictures and structures of time, a grace light transfigures us, blinds us to new sight. Our Caher Island face offers us this one lonely trust. Victory and success in the known world is not guaranteed. The hosts of power stamp on the powerless moments of insight and love. The deathsquads of interest plough under the harvests of plenty for the poor. Weapons cut the meek fields of wheat to a blackened earth. The sobs of an oppressed people, third worlders, the half-world of women, itinerants, the sick and dying, the old and homeless, are not heard over the loudspeaker demands of profit and gain. The voice for justice and peace is lost under the bellows of ideology and death.

Yet what hope we have is found in the crucified Christ. Against the darkening of the future he utters his way out. From the Caher Cross we can hear the minimal sentences of hope. These last words draw the breath of the future; the silence between each phrase creates a new space to live in, a new air to breathe. A cry of thirst for even bitter vintage against the hungry grass. Words of forgiveness for those who hammer nails into flesh, inviting the blind violent eyes to see the tears of the suffering. A promise of paradise for those who, in their own hell of death, reach out to another's pain. A care for a mother and friend become the home of a community of hope. As the night intensifies around him, inside him, he feels the abandonment of God, the forsaken isolation of spirit. His words then caress the extremity of the human despair under indifferent clouds. With nothing left, emptied of everything, he abandons himself to an abandoning God. The Caher Island face still says its frail words of an accomplished life and sets itself towards the open sea of the future. A trust in that face before every human heart that finds its lonely truth. Two thousand years since Calvary, one thousand five hundred years since Caher stone thrived, those words still echo from the world. The pain and darkness of that moment still wrench the mind and body. The exiled Christ is one who identifies with the exiled humans. Cut off from God, from family, from community, from health and joy and yet insisting on the necessity of life lived utterly to its even lowest point. Out of this necessity comes Caher Island itself. It arose from the cross. Caher Island has its first heartbeat at the edge of Calvary, over its precipice cliffs. It has its origin in that fresh moment when Christ stands in a spring garden and is mistaken, by Magdalene, for a gardener. This, to me, is the axis of time. For a fleeting, never-ending moment, they stand there together, a man and a woman. In a garden scented by early flowers, the palette of a new art and heart. They are the Adam and Eve of a new creation. In that encounter we sense the goodness, the ecstacy of Eden, the blessedness and goodness of all. This a redeemed earth and from that moment men and women and children share the world in concelebration of their gift and call. They are named to give life and love where there is hatred and death. To plant among the skulls of Calvary the seeds of rare flowers. It is no idle, easy call. For the Christ of those days is the Caher Island Christ. He bears on his body the woundings of the world. We can see the marks; the doubting are asked to touch. So there is no escape from the cross. Nor evasion of resurrection. The community that gathers in his name must never avoid the crucifixion of flesh. To remain with Christ is to remain with those who suffer, who hunger and thirst and cry out for love. To be true is to know deeply the atheist chill on the Golgotha hearts of many. To stay with Christ is to offer a way which will be open-handed to his beatitudes of compassion and care. The call from Calvary and Caher is for a community and world which is broken open to the battered God of love in every moment and person and thing. The cry in this place is for life, life in its fulness and wholeness. It asks for a fidelity to the creative urge of God and to the universe which was love spill of that urge. It begs a word and action of what it was like in the beginning and is now if we can find courage and faith.

When I visited Caher the place recalls me to our task and joy. And to the difficulties. I have come here after journeys to lands at war. From funerals in Northern Ireland which led to other funerals. Where guns were targetted on every living creature, and the mouths of people prayed litanies of hatred and superiority. On another occasion I walked the island after returning from El Salvador. Beside the graves of the monks on Caher, I remembered again the graves of Romero, priests, nuns, catechists, 50,000 peasants and workers in the merciless dumps of their country, and in the Caher face of Christ heard again the words of Christ spoken afresh and new in the eyes of the El Salvadorians who dared to read their scripture in the burning land. This suffering one says clearly, 'Thou shalt not kill.' 'Those who live by the sword die by the sword.'

Twice in deep winter I made landing on Caher. Both times to honour friends with the benediction of its solitude. Once with Fr Daniel Berrigan, S.J., whose laughter and words and gestures first brought me to priesthood and whose continued presence to life in friendship and love remain one of life's greatest gifts. He carried with him to Caher his years in American jails opposing Vietnam war and the nuclear madness of today. To balance this he carried, lightly, the poetry of a lifetime, the gentle, ecstatic words of a world loved. Later he wrote of that visit: 'Clinging to their inhospitable island like sea birds to a cliff, lost to the world and its iron ways, seeking in solitude the spirit of wisdom and self-knowledge, what a healing the monks offered – and offer. Yin and yang, faith and compassion, gathering into one the fragments of a soul, fragments of community, they made peace with the warring halves of our humanity, whose divisions and wounds are our present travail. Fourteen centuries later, the monks may even have worked such healing for me.'

Another winter visit brought another healing. The then retired Bishop Hanson came to Clare Island in the hope of seeing Caher. We waited two days for the journey out. Two days of storm and bitter wind. During these hours he spoke, reluctantly, of the events in Northern Ireland, of his stand against the paramilitaries on the Unionist side and the consequences of that on his life. More eagerly he spoke eloquently and passionately about St Patrick, to whose life and writing he was dedicated. As he spoke we could see the hard edges of his Croagh and prose, pointing to God. On the first morning he attended Mass. Next day I asked would he like to receive communion. 'Yes.' Later that day we scrambled up the stone beach of Caher. The legend of a Patrician foundation bound us together as we touched the stones, and traced the face. The winds seemed to scatter the centuries of division in the Christian churches and the face draw them into one. The island submitted us to the Christ who is with and beyond both our traditions. Next morning, before leaving, with joy we concelebrated together. The journey to Caher was indeed a healing.

Other friends were there at other times. Many loved ones who find no home in the church they long to be part of. Women especially, who judge the position of women in the Catholic church to be deeply insulting and hurtful. And will have none of it. They risk themselves instead to the struggle for their own freedom. If the church is to live truthfully it must go nakedly before their accusation, be washed clean in the salt water of womens' tears. Every Eucharist we say must be riven by these hard questions. To make real the incarnate Christ is to be present to the call of the time we live in. The breakthroughs of every age, the insights often granted in pain, must be the opening of new doors, the closure of prison cells. The barbarity of this century's wars, the dark shadow of Hiroshima and Nagasaki have re-opened us to the non-violence of Christ. A diplomatic 'just-war' theory lies under the ruin of many cities. In this age we have witnessed the beginning of the end of empires, the reclaiming of native lands and rights. Too often the churches had been part of the conquest. The cross, the bomb, and sword in easy alliance. We are having to face the dark consequences of that treaty. A racism, a cultural and ecclesiastical imperialism have deep roots by now. Slowly indigenous words and rhythms and colours return. The church is being enriched day by day by this liberation of suppressed people and thoughts. And freed of its chaplaincy to the greed of power. Today the biggest question facing us is that of women. Their cry of exclusion is heard from every corner of the globe. By and large they have been excluded from economic, cultural, artistic, sexual, ecclesiastical power. In these and so many other areas their thoughts and ideas have been marginalised. The consequences of this for women are beyond doubt – poverty, powerlessness, brutality, quiet and loud despair, joylessness, loneliness. Men have also lost much from this, both as individuals and as collectives. They have been formed by the prevailing cultures to deny and bury so much love and compassion. Their minds and imaginations have been denied the fruition of the feminine. Their sexuality, in language and act, is seen as conquest and power. For both men and women the years ahead will be difficult. Centuries of slavery and degradation leave wounds and scars not easily healed. Thought patterns lie deeper than blood. Within the Catholic church, thought is male, and celibate male. This leaves a deep imbalance, a cloistered feel.

To live with such thoughts is not easy. So many dear friends feel removed from the church to which I belong. I hear their anger and their pain and disappointment. I know it deepest in the Eucharist, that meal eaten on the edge of trials and death with friends' care and love. In the Eucharist the passionate time has its hour, the brutalities and crucifixions of every age are expressed. The priest stands there with energies of a place, dark and bright ones, offering a healing. Today, in the force-field of feminist thought I find myself, with many other priests, doing an act forbidden to my mother, my sister, friends and relatives who have granted me love and words, music and art, the everyday generosities of humour and care. I touch the apartheid altar, afraid. To risk some sexist language might be, sadly, appropriate. It is as if the bread of male daily labour is offered freely and openly, but the blood of a woman's full life and love is forbidden its place and celebration. There is an anaemic pain in this. A loss whose depth we cannot measure in church and society. There is a moment of healing in every sacrament. When we are touched by the creative God. 'In the image of God he made us, male and female.' God's image and reality is the union of the male and female. And the dream of every sacrament is the reality of that communion. So we dream of a concelebration when a woman shares the altar, to make present that incarnate God in whom 'there is no more Greek or Jew, male or female, slave or free.' All must, we believe, be made one in Christ Jesus, all must share equally the gift and promise of that priesthood.

On Caher Island you live in the call of the future, the risk and daring of it. Here the unknown plays itself on you, the shifting shadows and colours of the surrounding hills of Mayo and Galway. The changing moods and music of the sea. I began my studies for the priesthood in the warm peasant embrace of John XXIII and the words of the Second Vatican Council. The church then seemed humble before the world and its call. Aware of its often bad history, it was able to find the words to speak to 'all men and women of good will'. It held out the possibility of forward journeys, in small currachs, to a future which might be made new, reconciled to peace, justice, union. Today there is a sense of other things. A tightening of the hatches on a liner moored in some forgotten port ... theologians seeking the wounded truths of the poor, writers expressing the anguish and abandonment of women, homosexuals, for instance – these and others hear the rattle of the warder's keys.

A church that seemed set for those truths which always lie over the horizons among the discarded ones, now comes across as a centralised, moribund body, wagging its finger, not opening its wounded hands. But the voices that matter cannot be stilled into silence. They reach us from the hovels of the poor, the prison cells of the regimes. 'The good will' of others touches us towards what Thomas Merton called 'an ecumenism of the world'. The conscience of the Reformation, the stillness of the East, the great spirit of Amerindian thought, the passionate love of many atheists for the earth and its people – all these and more draw us towards the God beyond naming, beyond law and our timid order. From within the church so many remain and celebrate their humanity and redemption and work with patient hope for other times.

With themes like these I find a strange home on Caher Island. I find echoes here which resound off past and future. For this island church had its origins in the deserts of Syria and Egypt. The old Irish word for such places is *díseart*. Desert. The words make a rhyme and poem out of that decision by the first monks to leave behind the boundaries of the Roman Empire. They walk across the borders of the powers that be. They refuse to be part of an empire which makes sacred the demands of the state. Their church had been seen as an enemy to all that. It had refused to bow before Caesar. It had not worn the armour of soldiery. Christ, they believed, had blessed the peace-makers, banished the swords of destruction and death. Now that same church was embraced by the empire. Over a battle field the cross had been seen. The killing of others was suddenly justified. The brotherhood and sisterhood of their community was developing the titles and dress of a caste state. They sought a return to the simplicities of Christ. In the deserts they sought the 'white martyrdom' of community and God. In their lives and stories they attempt the perfection of humanity. The monastic church, which originates Celtic Christianity, shared this dream. We can taste it yet, like good bread on hungry tongues, in their words and art. The monks of Caher Island came from tribes which were dedicated to the warrior creed, which protected and extended their reign over lands and people by sword. Their heroes are soldiers crowned in blood. The gospel of Christ came as challenge to this ideology of war. The monks heard it and dedicated themselves to this new peace. They left behind the sword. Their poetry makes clear the radicalness of the change and not merely this decision. There was something deeper involved. For they were not called to God alone. To share in God was to share in the earth. Their lives became a communion with the climate and geography, the biology and botany of Mayo. They found on the seas and islands, in wind and sun, in seal and leek, in mountain and its eagle, a pilgrimage to the living God. Out of all this came what I will call, for want of a better phrase, an 'Ecology of Salvation'. That phrase has the merit, at least, of not ringing the till of the much used 'economy of salvation'. The art and poetry, the life of those people, includes all in its benediction. The writing emerges with a clear, wind-swept air, a wild bird's poise and grace. God is everywhere. In the silence of their hearts they have heard God's voice in the whole of creation. Nothing is removed from the grace of such living. The song of the Lagan Blackbird, the wood creatures and plants of the Connacht hermit, Marbhán, are at home on the given earth. In the 'Breastplate of St Patrick' we are presented with a map of that world. It binds the trinity itself but also cherubim, angels, archangels, prayers, predictions, preachings, faith and deeds, the brightness of the snow, the splendour of fire, the speed of lightning, wind's cut, sea's depths, rock's solidity. It is an extraordinary poem to the unity of being, an ecology that bound together God, creation, humanity. Here lies the strength of that founding church. Here lies its clue to us in a time of uncertainty and fear.

A now uninhabited island is a Cassandra place. It oracles, amid the ruins of a rich civilisation, the possibility of an uninhabited earth. Primarily the warnings of a nuclear-winter, a lifeless planet under the cloud of death. To reverence the God of life, to embrace his creation, demands a life-long commitment to peace on earth. As the Caher monks rejected the arms of their tribes, we too must make decisions about our future. As each day passes, our neutrality as a nation is under attack. We are often drawn towards European defence arrangements. The bottom line of such defence is nuclear weaponry. So far we have remained free of such alliances. Or we like to think so. But there is some evidence that our seas are haunted by the shadow of nuclear submarines, that overhead planes fly, primed with the talons of missiles. Some voices within our nation argue the necessity of becoming involved in European defence. That madness must be faced with the sanity of refusal. And more than that. We must as a people be urgent in our voice and action to ensure the banning of all such weaponry from the earth. Neutrality before such evil is not negative. It is the nuclear-ridden nations who may neuter the world.

There are other threats. On the beach of Caher we have found hardwood, mollusced at sea, from the Amazon. An omen of that destruction of the lungs of the earth. From Caher this year I could see the new scar across the flank of Croagh Patrick as new greed prepared to break open the sacred place. On nearby islands the once rich earth is chewed to desolation by over-grazing. Today's grants ensure an empty future. The seas around Caher retain their bracing purity – but the spread of nuclear waste and poison pushes towards us. The damage may already be very deep, sinking slowly into the subterranean and submarine bloodcells of life itself. Our children may have to drink the poisoned waters, eat the lethal flesh. From the hermit monks we must learn that love of God must be one with love of humanity and the created universe. We cannot bow down before the creator while we destroy his creation.

At the heart of the Caher faith is the Trinity. Our tepid image is the hand of St Patrick bearing the shamrock. But there is a truth in this, deeper than the mathematics of three into one. A hard salutary lesson. Today the urgent direction of faith is centred on the humanity of Christ. This is a vital retrieval of his flesh, his identity with us in 'the ways of all flesh'. This counteracts a religion with only a distant God as its point, a religion which too often discards our anchor to reality. Or from the easy Alleluias of a pentecostalism which preaches false joy to hungry, oppressed people. On Caher Island, at our fingertips, is a full-blooded faith which is profoundly Trinitarian, which worshipped and lived out a belief in God, Spirit and Christ. This original faith of our fathers and mothers is vital to our future. The creator God makes place and space for the world, speaks its goodness over the days and nights of creation. Creator and creature are bound together in an act of love. Jesus Christ heals the wounds of nature and human choice and history. He restores us to our origins. And everywhere the Spirit is present in that recreation of the earth, in our response to beauty and terror, in daily wonder and discovery of our lives, in the urgings of the world towards peace and justice. Patrick's shamrock, or indeed every salted flower of Caher, is not some puerile metaphor for the Trinity, but indeed is the very Trinity itself. Because the restless God spills out into creation, and its water-mark is written deep in the fabric of all living things.

There discovery of this sacrednesss is the gift of this place and history. And it opens our future. Our daily bread today is eaten while reading newspaper accounts of the most recent murder in Northern Ireland. With the inevitable religious affiliation of the deceased. All sides have declared war. The ruling governments in Britain and the south have made war on 'the terrorists'. 'The freedom-fighters' of both sides are armed to the teeth against one another. Most people seem forced to choose between sides. To side with the powers that govern, or to give an active or tacit support to paramilitaries. Either way is to stand over graves, to nod one's head at the death of others. Very few seem prepared to venture a new thought, a new community based on ideals of truth and justice, of the sacredness of all, to beat the swords into the ploughshares of some new land. Both sides are victims of their history. British Unionism will not look the reality of a colonial past in its bloody eyes.

Irish Nationalism bears the scars of oppression and the hatreds and deaths of the struggle to change it. Behind both lie religions of exclusion, where street-corner dogmas and backwood catechisms declare the others to be lost, to be anti-Christ, to be not worthy of salvation. Before any new way forward can be found there must be a facing of the past. Not just the past of 'the otherside', but one's own bitter harvest of blood. The failure to do this today, allied to the death-toll of each week, makes one quake before the future. Every bullet fired today has a future repercussion. A deeper hardening of the arteries of our heart. History must reveal to all sides the grim reality that power, won or gained by violence, destroys the living also, as it destroyed the corpses of the Boyne, Abercorn, Enniskillen, Gibraltar. The spectre of the dead makes the future impossible for the living.

Religions, humanity, to remain true to themselves must rededicate their every moment to the sacred guardianship of each other's sacredness. To a deep love of different ways and traditions. For laws in the land which allow room for those we differ with, on such questions as divorce, marriage, schools and contraception. In the republic, some of us stood appalled at the time of the divorce referendum. Appalled for those bound under the suffocating weight and suffering of brutal and impossible marriages, desertions. Appalled for those religions who allow divorce, but are forbidden by Irish law to do so. Appalled for our own faith, which professes a Declaration of Religious Freedom.

This is but one example of an intolerance towards other views which eats at the heart of our country. The homelessness of so many people, the inability to deal openly and worthily with homosexuality, the development of a medical system which gives precedence to those with money. There is a cynicism and despair in many minds. Once more emigration, which begins to denude the West of its best hope. Some going because of economic necessity, many others in search of freedoms not given at home. There is around us a deepening growth in suicide. Much of our education system trims the sail of learning to the narrow rudder of monetarist economics. Minds and arts and sensibilities, which might explore with the churches the human dilemma and vocation, are ringed against us.

I have no solutions to such problems. The anger and darkness is within me also. But on Caher Island there is a first balm of healing. It touches the leper skin of all creation with open hands. And that face offers us the invitation to walk the human journey with grace. To know and find the goodness of every living moment. To wine the nuptial days, to touch the diseased body with love, to walk across the borders of hatred, to bring the fulness of life to all threatened by local and universal death. To know, in the bone's marrow, in the spirit's sap, in the soul's blood, that only the compassionate face reaches across time.

Forever on the Periphery
Pádraig Standún

I am in Inis Meáin, the middle, or should I say, central island of Aran in Galway Bay. I sit on the cliff edge on the west side of the island, which is off the edge of Ireland, itself off the edge of Europe. I feel that I am sitting on the edge of the world.

This is my favourite place in the world, my spiritual home. Great waves thunder at the butt of the sheer cliff, green water exploding white on slimy brown birdshitted rock. Salt spray soars to the clifftop and spits on my page. There is no 'master' to rage at my inkspots.

I must have been a seagull here once. Did I see Spanish sails sink over the western horizon? Is there any truth in the rumour that Columbus names the 'Pinta' after the fine *pionta* he had in Inis Meain? Anything is possible. After all the Sound below me is named after a Pope, Gregory the Great. There is a cave named after him too. Some caveman!

I speak *ex cathedra* from this clifftop — which is nothing new in this diocese (Tuam). Didn't John McHale say that every parish priest in his Archdiocese considered himself infallible? He was explaining that he had no real difficulty with papal infallibility, despite being one of the six bishops who voted against its proclammation at the 1870 Vatican Council. There has always been a sneaking feeling that the McHale vote gave his diocese some lee way in the matter of questioning. Which may go some way towards explaining the existence of this book, McHale being a Mayoman whose two dioceses covered most of the county.

The particular *cathedra* that I speak *ex*, is named after a dramatist as familiar with Gaoth Saile as with Inis Meáin — John Millington Synge. Synge's chair is a halfcircle of stones in which he found shelter and inspiration. One day he met one of my predecessors whom he described as 'wet and worn out, coming to have his first meal'. (*The Aran Islands*, p 146) The priest had been brought across the rough sea, fasting since midnight, between Masses in Inis Oirr and Inis Meáin. 'Well, begob, Mr Synge,' he said, 'if you ever go to heaven, you'll have a great laugh at us.' Synge's spirit often meets me on the cliff. We both laugh.

There is a contentment here, *suaimhneas*, that quality we so desire for our dead — *suaimhneas síoraí*, so much stronger than 'eternal rest'. I can be relaxed here, even with God.

It is not that I argue divine existence from the beauty of this place, from the beauty of the world. True, I have dissected God, argued the toss and tossed the arguments. I have scalpelled the entrails, sliced them as thin as theological distinctions, found everything and nothing. The sublime has been indifferent to my poking and probing.

Yet, I feel I have known grace. God has touched me. No dramatics. No burning bush. No Damascus. People mainly.

For me it all started in the low bog-spaced drumlins of central Mayo, a February mushroom under a head of spring cabbage. A happy childhood. Faith was not forced, just imbibed, nurtured in the home and in Clogher school. A tall priest with a shock of white hair came to the school and told us stories, Bible stories, Grimm brothers stories, a mixture of both sometimes, maybe. He spellbound his listeners. As I listened to the Jesus-stories, I could not imagine that Jesus would speak with anything but the voice of Tommy Gibbons. Somewhere I had heard of a priest's hands being anointed. I assumed that it was holy oil rather than chain-smoked Sweet Aftons (the packet with the poem – typically) that yellowed Tommy's fingers.

We went to Mass by horse and trap. Fanny was a black mare with a white face and four white anklesocks. The black cross on my rosary beads had a white figure of the crucified Christ. This immediately became the horse's face. Fanny spent many a Mass jumping over the board at the back of the seat in front of me. Religion can be fun.

Tommy Gibbon's sermons were not always Jesus-stories either. He told one Sunday of a piece of meat he got from the butcher. After frying, boiling and roasting had failed to make it edible, he said it would have been more suitable for half-soling shoes. I'm sure the butcher got the message.

He was never made a parish priest. When asked one day what had brought him to town, he said that he was celebrating the feast of the passover – his turn for a parish had come and gone. Replying to an invitation to the official opening of an extension to his *alma mater*, he said it was rather like the type of perk offered to the leader of the opposition. An exceptional, if somewhat eccentric man. A great priest.

Religion was anything but a morose puritanical set of prohibitions. There was always laughter, and I was blessed with parents who were as full of wit as of wisdom. Other relatives too.

Kate, my father's sister had arthritis. She was in pain as long as I knew her. She buried her husband when her only daughter, Nellie was three. Nellie died before she was thirty, leaving her mother to rear her own children. Things were rough on the land. Cattle died of blackleg. Prices were poor, money scarce. Kate never lost her faith or her humour. Job should have been a woman.

Kathleen, my mother's sister had nine children. She was in a wheelchair twenty years when she died at sixty. Her husband, Paddy died a young man. She, too, was as full of humour as she was of faith. Full of grace. How heaven must ring with their laughter. Almighty crack.

Despite that faith background, or because of it, I belong to the periphery of the Roman Catholic Church as much as I belong to the edge of Europe. A quintessential *à la carte* Catholic, I have been on the losing side in the major Church/State referenda conflicts of the eighties. I think the church mistaken on the question of contraception, unjust in the matter of women's rights, downright silly in the matter of compulsory clerical celibacy. None of those attitudes prevents me from being a priest of the church. Questioning, seeking change from the inside is part of my loyalty to and love of the church. I have no major problems with the essentials of the faith. I can say the creed without blushing. The matters questioned, while of great importance in themselves and a great burden to many people, are peripheral to faith in God and in Jesus Christ.

'A la carte Catholic' has become a term of abuse, an in-phrase used to disparage the conscientious choices made by the people of God. I would look on it as a badge of honour, and substitute 'à la Críost Christian.' Jesus was an 'à la carte Jew'. The letter of the law was of lesser importance to him than an approach of love and compassion.

Speaking of cart(e)s I have heard some of his fellow carpenters suggest that Joseph was less than a credit to his profession in not making a cart(e) to take Mary to Bethlehem. We did have a cart to put out the turf. It was pulled by a black jackass with no reverse in his repertoire. Which brings me back to Mayo, to cutting the umbilical earth-chord which tied me to the land of my father's and mother's people.

The symbolic act I most associate with leaving the land was cutting the turfbank for the last time. Generations before me had cut a straight sod to keep out the water the next year. My father had died. I had put my hand to the plough. The place was sold. I was the last of the line to wield a *sleán* there. I hacked brutally and indiscriminately at the soft underbelly of the bog, a tearing out of roots. Any radicalism in me was born in that boghole. As we climbed the last hill home, Paddy Fahy, who was cutting in co with me said, 'It will be a long time before you and me cut turf together again.' I never handled a sleán since.

Circumstances have brought me back to the language of some at least of my great grandparents. My mother's grandmother was the last person to go to confession on a regular basis in Irish in Balla. The curate, later Parish Priest in Aran, An tAth Tomás Ó Cillín was an Irish language enthusiast, so they used have great conversations. The family had moved in a Congested District Board's change from the foot of Nephin to clear the whins from newly divided land by the railway line beyond Balla. The Irish language and the poteen-making were left behind. New wine in the new wineskins. The faith of the McHale country they brought with them, however.

It is in Irish I write as I attempt to weave parables for the present time. An attempt too to deal with questions of faith and morality, to make some sense for myself and hopefully for others. Writing a second language, a learned language, has difficulties, but also advantages. There is a certain discipline involved in not being able to use big polthógs of lazy catchall words. Remember Synge's statement of not having used more than two words he had not heard in the mouths of the people. This is important when someone writes propaganda rather than literature, parable rather than philosophy.

Stories, particularly novels, give a person room to deal with a broad sweep of life, to define attitudes, to see how you might come to terms with a particular situation. They do not tell you how to live, so much as let you make your own decisions. 'She/he who has ears to hear...'

This is an attempt to follow the methods of Jesus. Do not insist. Do not force. Do not pressurise. Call. Invite. Suggest. Tell stories. Take it or leave it stories. Understanding the difficulty stories. Love and consequences stories. Allowing for all possibilities stories. As a priest, the main thing is to get the point across, particularly to your own parishioners, that you try to understand, that nothing shocks you, that you have heard it all before, that all can be forgiven, that God is good, that people are human, and the priest more human than most.

Sometimes stories shock for a while. There is a nine day wonder. Fellow clergy 'tut tut'. People ask, 'How did he get to know about that?' The reward is when someone comes to you and says, 'I read such and such and felt you would understand.'

So far I have written four novels, two published, a third ready for publication, the fourth at the rewriting stage. Themes are of the edge, of the periphery of life, the periphery of religion, about people's attempt to live, to come to terms with life and with God in situations not of their own making for the most part. They are about survival in the face of life as it is idealised, mainly by churches, and as it is lived in reality.

Súil le Breith deals with clerical celibacy in the context of life on an island. It also deals with the struggle with the sea, the effects of emigration, and people's attempt to make a better life for themselves. *Ad 2016* looks at what life in Ireland could be like on the hundredth anniversary of the 1916 Rising, if attitudes prevalent in society today are taken to their logical conclusions. The third, as yet unnamed, novel deals with the Gaeltacht sometime in the nineties while also being a homosexual and specifically lesbian love story. *Bidín* is about an old recluse who has rejected society since the day she was read from the altar for being single and pregnant. Her mother broke the handle of the brush on her back. She now lives in squalid conditions in a hut on the bog and her situation is beginning to prick the collective conscience of the local social services committee. Read on ...

What I am really saying is, go out and buy and read these books if you want to know where I stand in regard to humanity and God. They are my testament. They say what I am unable to say in these few pages, because I am too old, too long living and reading between the lines to put in straightforward language where God and I stand in relation to each other. Anyway there is no black and white, and when did God ever stand still?

God is the seagull now, swooping, swaying, soaring above the cliff edge. No strings. No puppet master/mistress this God. A God of freedoms. Reluctant maybe, how she would love to gather her chickens under her wing, but she has to let them go, let them take their chances as they drop from the cliff wall nest.

Life is not all about the seagull on the cliff, the mad monk on the rock. The retreat to the desert, to the deserted creig is necessary though to see life in perspective, to deal with the harsh realities of island life. Claustrophobic isolation hits some more than others, affects born islanders as much as blow-ins like myself. Small issues can become big, molehills mountains. There is constant danger, danger for currach fishermen riding high on Atlantic waves. So much for the benefits of European Communion – we sit on one of the finest fisheries in the community, and fish from currachs, because Inis Oirr or Inis Meáin have no safe harbours.

There is flying fear generated from almost exclusive dependence on an air service, especially in winter. It is no use telling us that flying is one of the safest means of transport. That's me up there in the plane, and my number might be just coming up. Not to speak of the pilot's number.

An island is the world in miniscule. Sometimes old and new complement each other. At other times there is inevitable tension between tradition and progress, between conservatism and change-or-die attitudes, between gombeenism and cooperativism. Purveyors of the diplomatic trade could benefit a lot from a spell on an island before tackling problems like the Middle East, for instance.

Popes and prelates should be sent to the islands too, to see deep faith and generosity in action, to see the response when someone is lost at sea or in danger, to see the value of life, to see people risk their lives for others. Lifeboatmen, doctors, nurses, currach crews, facing boiling seas with a stretcher-patient in labour strapped to the seats, bringing an expectant mother to the lifeboat. Here in the islands the thirteenth station of the cross is very real. Too many mothers have, pietà-like, held the cold bodies of drowned children, most mothers much younger than Synge's Maura as usually played in *Riders to the Sea*. This is life in all its raw reality.

There has been steady, footslogging progress in community development on the islands, mainly through the cooperatives and despite the devastation of emigration. There is always the hope that some at least, having seen and learned from the wide world, will return with fresh and positive ideas. Many rural west of Ireland communities could learn a lot from the islands about community development.

Liberation theology is a reality rather than a catchphrase here. There is a realisation that no one out there is going to help us unless we try and help ourselves. Government agencies can and will help, but the demand and the cooperation must come from the people. Solidarity is built as people of the islands march through Galway in the rain on Holy Saturday demanding a proper and long-promised ferry service. No need for fancy words of theological justification. The reality is there. Small scale, but real.

I write as an exile (neither silent or cunning) far from the county Mayo. No evidence that Galway has been glad to get what Mayo begat. My little contribution has had to do with pastoral theology in pen and practice. I have every reason to be modest with regard to theology – only a Mayoman would have dreamt of asking me to contribute to a book on the subject. It's not so much, 'Mayo God help us' with me, as 'God and Mayo forgive me.'

A Passionate God?

Enda McDonagh

A passionate God sounds unlikely. Pure spirit, absolute being, unmoved mover, immutable and impassible; no room for emotion or passion there. Anyway the whole idea has proved very dangerous. War in the name of God testifies to the long history of destructive religious passion. Such passion is still with us. The great religions of the Book and of the God of the Book, Judaism, Christianity and Islam, as well as Hinduism and Buddhism, are still provoking, and at times endorsing, destructive passion. Every night the television screen carries the implicit warning that religious passion could endanger your health and that of whole societies. Armenia and Azerbajan, Israel and the West bank, Punjab and Sri Lanka, the Ukraine and Northern Ireland, with the broader international threats of sabotage and assassination, in the name of Allah or whatever, all underline the savage energy released by religious passion.

For all that, passion is an essential component of human being, of human living and of human creativity. Our discernment of God, however intellectual it may appear, can never be separated from the passionate energy which enters into our search for truth, as it does into every other human activity. Even the most dried up academic is motivated by some passionate desire for truth or prestige or promotion or power. Outside academia, the passion-play, in human creative and constructive activity, is at least as obvious as it is in dangerous and destructive activity. In religion too the creators and innovators have been people of passion. From Abraham through Moses to Jesus and beyond, the passions of creative energy, of human sympathy, suffering and endurance, have established a pattern of leaders passionately engaged, at the call of God, in prayer and in the service and liberation of their fellows. The history of divine-human relations in the Jewish and Christian Scriptures has a succession of passionate people who speak with God and for God. The Jewish ideal king David, the prophets of harsh denunciation like Amos, or of love and promise like Isaiah, all contribute to a gallery of the crucially committed. The passionate are preferred to those who are neither 'cold nor hot'. 'So because you are lukewarm and neither cold nor hot I will spew you out of my mouth.' (Rev 3:15-16)

The passion of God's people, in its creative and in its destructive forms, enters into our understanding not only of humanity but also of God. As far as the literature of the Hebrews goes, the passion of God – anger, jealousy, vengeance, forgiveness, generosity and above all love in its intimate, creative and seeking forms – is as clearly and regularly recorded as human passion is. The rejection of all this in the name of anthropomorphism, the uncritical application of human characteristics to God, is not convincing. The Hebrews maintained a very firm and clear idea of the transcendence of God and were not so naïve in their attributions as sometimes alleged. This will become clear later, I hope. Despite the famous restraint of the New Testament in speaking of God, it still reveals a passionate and compassionate Father-God in love with the world to the point of sending and sacrificing his own Son.

A Manner of Speaking
Human creation in the image of God has proved a rich source of reflection on the nature of God. All that is peculiarly human in terms of intellect and will, of freedom, love and justice, of truth and fidelity, has been recognised and accepted as applicable to God in a manner free from creaturely limitations. This manner of speaking of the characteristics of God has been called analogical or proportional, where the proportions between finite creature and infinite creator have to be kept in mind. Other human attributes, such as personal and spiritual, are applied in the same analogical way. God is spiritual or personal in a way similar to human beings but also dissimilar. Our manner of speaking about God then is valid in attaining to a knowledge of God, as long as we respect the limitations, sometimes expressed as similarity in dissimilarity or identity in difference. The meaning of God remains deeply obscure. And for some theologians the rules of the game are more helpful in determining what we may not say about God, than in endorsing what we may say.

Examples of this prohibition on certain language about God includes body and, its associate, emotion. God is pure spirit, unlike the human being. So God does not occupy space, does not age and die, does not feel or suffer. Whatever happens in the historical interchange between God and humanity affects and changes us. It does not affect and change God.

God transcends history and humanity and the changes to which they are subject. Along this line of argument, very widely accepted by Christians everywhere, there would seem to be no question of passion in God either. Passion and passionate would not seem to be allowed under the rules of analogy. This very strong argument is not a strictly Jewish and Christian argument. Indeed the ordinary reading of the bible would suggest a certain passion, creative and enduring, not only about Abraham, Moses and Jesus but also about their God. Language-watching in relation to God has been deeply influenced by Greek and other philosophical traditions. Not that the Jews or early Christians were exactly careless, but they did rejoice in a proliferation of images and metaphors about God which some later more philosophical theologians found difficult to include in their systematic God-talk. Intellectual power and sophistication were not always able to stop theologians, as gifted as St Thomas Aquinas, from discussing God in rather arid and abstract terms. Lesser intellects found such abstractness even more congenial so that the God of Old and New Testaments became the unmoved and immovable first mover, at very many removes from the emotional and mutable human beings, created in God's image and out of God's love. A serious gulf existed and continues to exist between the God of a certain theology, and the God of the bible and of people's prayer. In a Mayo book of theology, where the people's prayer and the bible are essential sources for understanding and speaking about God, the limitations of purely abstract theology must be examined. Some richer vision of God is required to match the testimony of the faithful from the hungry grass.

A Passionate Creation
The passion which is native to human beings enters into their creative activities. This is most evident in their sexual creativity. The most basic human activities of sexual loving and life-giving are considered among the most passionate of human activities and by some people as the only passionate ones. This partly accounts for the hesitancy about using the word passion at all in theology. Other creative human activities depend on passion as energiser. This applies obviously to the world of politics, to establishing and maintaining a free and just society. Passion for justice or freedom has been one of the distinctive features of heroic human figures in everybody's history. Without that intensity of conviction and engagement of energy which constitutes the passionate politician, very little progress in justice and freedom would ever have been achieved. And one could go on through explorers, scientists, artists and religious founders to confirm the need for passion in all serious creative achievement.

Human creativity derives for Christians from the divine. The conviction, commitment and energy which characterises limited human creation has its source in that first act of divine creation. It is impossible to read the biblical accounts of universal creation, for example in Genesis (1,2) or Job (38), without recognising a passionate creator at work. The commitment and energy, the joy, the indignation and the sorrow, all bespeak a creator passionately involved with his creation. Such talk may be dangerous. All God-talk is. Yet it seems as justified in proportional or analogical terms as saying God is merciful or forgiving or just. The conviction and energy-engagement of human passion are harnessed creatively by the whole human, reasoning being. It is hard to describe adequately how the reasoning and passionate human forms a critical unity. Yeats foresees that darkest of times when 'the best lack all conviction and the worst are full of compassionate intensity'. In the unity of God, the conviction and intensity cohere with the divine intelligence, reason and knowledge. More explicit discussion of God's relations with the created world, cosmos and humanity may help to clarify that.

The Sea, The Sea

The roar and tumult of Atlantic wind and sea can settle quickly. Storm and calm come in succeeding waves. The passion of raw energy suddenly gives way to passionate, throbbing peace. The coast of Mayo bears the marks and scars of that wind and sea. So do many of its people. They share these marks and scars with other and older communities. Seas and storms have been inspiring and frightening humanity since its origins. In Jewish and Christian faith they have been symbols of the creative and terrifying power of God. The Spirit of God, which moved over the face of the waters in the Hebrew picture of creation (Gen 1:2), conveyed something of the conviction and energy, of the passion of Yahweh, Creator and Lord of the heavens and the earth. In Hebrew, as in Irish tradition, faith in God is rooted in closeness to land and sea. Nature poetry becomes expression of faith. And it is a passionate poetry. The God of creation deserves no less. The psalmist frequently speaks in passionate praise of the God of creation. Psalm 19 is typical and one of the best known:

> The heavens are telling the glory of God;
> and the firmament proclaims his handiwork.
>
> In them he has set a tent for the sun,
> which comes forth like a bridegroom leaving his chamber,
> and like a strong man runs its course with joy.

A more Atlantic note is struck in Psalm 93:

> The floods have lifted up, O Lord,
> the floods have lifted up their voice,
> the floods lift up their roaring.
> Mightier than the thunders of many waters,
> mightier than the waves of the sea,
> the Lord on high is mighty.

It is however in response to Job that the passion of Godself as Creator and Lord properly emerges. Indignantly comes the voice of the Lord out of the whirlwind (also a passionate image):

> Who is this that darkens counsel by words without knowledge?

> Where were you when I laid the foundation of the earth?
> Tell me if you have understanding.
> Or who shut in the sea with doors, when it burst forth from the womb;
> when I made the cloud its garment and thick darkness its swaddling band,
> and presribed bounds for it, and set bars and doors,
> and said, 'Thus far shall you come, and no farther,
> and here shall your proud waves be stayed?' (Job 38:2-11)

The intimate concern of God for creation enters deeply into the spirituality and teaching of Jesus. Many of his parables from the world of farming, fishing and shepherding, express his familiarity with the natural world and his care for it. Episodes like the stilling of the storm, the walking on the waters and the miraculous draft of fishes, emphasise his identity with the creative and caring power of God. This power of the Father in all its creativity and caring is marvellously summarised in a famous passage in the Sermon on the Mount, the charter of the new Kingdom or, as Paul calls it, the New Creation. While Jesus' main concern is with the foolish preoccupations of humanity, he incidentally reveals the passionate care of the Father for all his creatures.

> Therefore I tell you, do not be anxious about your life, what you shall eat or what you shall drink, nor about your body, what you shall put on ... Look at the birds of the air; they neither sow nor reap nor gather into barns, and yet your heavenly Father feeds them. Consider the lilies of the field, how they grow; they neither toil nor spin; yet I tell you, even Solomon in all his glory was not arrayed as one of these. (Mt 6: 25-30)

The early Irish monks reflected a similar sense of the natural world as God's gift and care and presence. Gerard Murphy entitles a ninth century monastic verse 'The Lord of Creation'.

> Adram in Coimdid
> cusnaib aicdid amraib,
> nem gelmar co n-ainglib,
> ler tonnban for talmain.

Thomas Kinsella translates:

> Adore we the Lord
> and his wonderful works:
> great Heaven bright with angels,
> Earth's sea white with waves.

A more expansive prayer and nature poem is the reply by the hermit Marbhán to King Guaire, also from the ninth century. Again I use Kinsella's translation to these extracts.

Marbhán:
I have a hut here in the wood
that nobody knows but my Lord.
An ash tree one side is its wall,
the other a hazel, a great rath tree.

Fresh spring wells
and falls of water
delicious to drink
break forth in plenty
with yew-tree berries,
and cherry and privet.

I render thanks
for what is given
by Christ in his goodness.

In 'Ealing Broadway, London Town,' Patrick Kavanagh recreates his own Monaghan hermitage.

Morning, the silent bog
And the God of imagination waking
In a Mucker fog.

Mayo's seas and bogs also provide fitting theatres for the God of imagination.

The passion of Kavanagh and of the hermit-poet for their native natural world is part of an older and continuing tradition of poetry. Poets are by nature passionate even when they are not being passionate about nature. The energy, conviction and inspiration which shapes a poet, amount to passion, however tempered and channelled. Nature poetry, as expression of religious faith and worship, is also older and broader than the Hebrew and Irish traditions. That all this should reflect the creative energy and commitment of God in the making of World and Word has about it the logic of Christian (and Jewish) faith. The further step of describing this creative energy and commitment of God in terms of God's passion may seem more difficult to some believers. Yet the Scriptures and their creative Christian imitators and commentators suggest just that. The theological safeguard of proportion or analogy would protect against the inevitable dangers of abuse. That danger might seem to arise more easily where the passion of erotic love is adopted as a way into understanding and expressing not just our love for God but God's love for us. Yet the Scriptures themselves and the great Christian mystics do not avoid such risks as we shall now see.

Intimacy and Inclusivity

God's steadfast love for his people forms a constant refrain in the Book of Psalms. It might be said to be the theme song of the whole bible, Old and New Testaments. Psalm 89 begins:

I will sing of thy steadfast love, O Lord, for ever:
with my mouth I will proclaim thy faithfulness to all generations.

The sober language and imagery of the psalms makes clear the daily and detailed care of God for the people of Israel and indeed for all people. The passion is in the detail. It emerges, more strongly in other descriptions of the relation between God and Israel. Hosea's enacted parable of this loving husband God and his faithless wife Israel provokes passionate declarations of love from God.

When the Lord first spoke through Hosea, the Lord said to Hosea, 'Go take to yourself a wife of harlotry and have children of harlotry, for the land commits great harlotry by forsaking the Lord' ... After the rejection and the punishment for infidelity comes the fresh wooing. Although 'she went after lovers and forgot me says the Lord ... behold I will allure her into the wilderness and speak tenderly to her ... And there she shall answer as in the days of her youth, as at the time she came out of the land of Egypt.' (Hos 1,2)

In chapter 3, Hosea recounts a second and similar call in terms stressing once again the depth and intimacy of God's love. And the

Lord said to me, 'Go again, love a woman who is beloved of a paramour and is an adulteress; even as the Lord loves the people of Israel, though they turn to other gods ...' (3:1)

The transcendent God of the Hebrew and Christian Scriptures, the totally other or the Holy One of Israel, clearly transcended the sexual duality of humanity and other biological beings. In this Yahweh differed from gods of neighbouring peoples. This was not because the Hebrews found anything wrong with sexuality. It was part of the goodness of all creation as the Genesis accounts emphasise. These accounts relate the sexual duality of humanity with its loving and life-giving capacities, directly to human dignity as created in the image of God. Maintaining this balancing act, no sexuality in God yet human sexual loving and creating as God-like, is one of the great achievements of Israel and its Scriptures.

The balancing act becomes more delicate with the integration into the Scriptures of the *Song of Songs*, a collection of erotic love-lyrics, and with their traditional interpretation as exemplifying the intimacy and engagement of Yahweh with his people. We have already seen how Hosea draws on sexual, marital loving to explore the relationship of God and Israel. This is featured elsewhere in the Old Testament and adopted in the New.

Jesus as bridegroom in the gospels (Mt 9:15) and the great marital mystery of Christ and the church in Ephesians 5, confirm the intimacy and intensity of the love between God and humanity. It is however the language of the *Song of Songs* which offers the closest parallel to later Christian mystics like John of the Cross as the struggle to express their love-experience of God. The biblical songs resemble in structure and tone John's 'Songs between the soul and the bridegroom'. And the erotic imagery is unmistakeable:

> *The Song of Songs*
>
> The voice of my beloved!
> Behold, he comes
> leaping over the mountains,
> bounding over the hills ...
> Upon my bed at night
> I sought him whom my soul loves ...
> Behold, you are beautiful my love ...
> Your lips are like a scarlet thread,
> and your mouth is lovely ...
> Your two breasts are like two fawns,
> twins of a gazelle,
> that feed among the lilies. (Song of Songs: 1-4)

St John of the Cross: 'Songs between the soul and the bridegroom':

> *Bride*
>
> Where can your hiding be,
> Beloved, that you left me thus to moan
> While like the stag you flee
> Leaving the wound with me?
> I followed calling loud but you had flown ...
>
> Oh who my grief can mend?
> Come, make the last surrender that I yearn for,
>
> Now flowers the marriage bed
> With dens of lions fortified around it,
> With tent of purple spread
>
> He gave his breast; seraphic
> In savour was the science he taught;
> And there I made my traffic
> Of all, withholding naught,
> And promised to become the bride he sought.
>
> (*Translation by Roy Campbell, Penguin 1980*)

A PASSIONATE GOD? 171

The relationship between God and Soul has in this mystic vision all the intensity and intimacy of human sexual loving while still respecting the transcendence of God. In this, as in God's wider relationships with his people, the description 'passionate' applies.

God's wider relationships remain supremely important. Unlike human passion, God's passion for humanity is not exhausted by one or a few powerful relationships. In the creation stories, as in the prophets, God's love extends to all humanity. This universality and inclusivity of God's love are central to the gospels, to the birth, life, death and resurrection of God's Son in Jesus Christ. Only a passionate God could be capable of such intimacy and inclusivity.

Hunger and thirst for Justice

The inclusivity which characterises God's love for human beings is opposed to all discrimination and oppression between them. It seeks justice for all. The centrality of justice to the bible, and its origins in God's own dealings with humankind is such a commonplace of contemporary theology that it needs little fresh development.

The divine passion for justice, as it could well be described, emerges clearly in Old and New Testaments. Those who hunger and thirst for justice are truly disciples. In such disciples can one trace further dimensions of the divine commitment and energy in overcoming the barriers between religion, race, class and gender. (Gal 3:28)

The overthrow of the mighty and the exalting of the humble, sketched in the Magnificat and elsewhere in the gospels, as well as in the prophets and psalms, outlines the divine strategy in the search for justice. Such a strategy has been badly needed in Mayo and in myriad similar deprived areas. In the depth of Mayo's privations in the 1870s and 1880s, the search for justice found effective expression in the Land League and its founder Michael Davitt. His life and teaching offer an insight into human hunger and thirst for justice. In line with the argument advanced here, such human hunger and thirst originates in the divine engagement of a passionate God and reveals that passion.

Christ of Passion and of Poetry

Have this mind among yourselves, which is yours in Christ Jesus ,who, though he was in the form of God, did not count equality with God a thing to be grasped, but emptied himself, taking the form of a servant, being born in the likeness of men. And being found in human form he humbled himself and became obedient unto death, even death on a cross. *(Paul's Letter to the Philippians 2: 5-8)*

The Passion of Christ is a very familiar devotional and theological expression. This is the passion of suffering, of enduring destruction rather than the passion of the human or of the divine creator. Some New Testament scholars have spoken of the gospels as primarily Passion Narratives with introductions on birth and ministry and conclusions on Resurrection attached later. It is however the gospels as a whole we have to deal with here, whatever the stages of their composition. The Passion Narratives remain crucial in our search for God. What kind of God would send his own Son to lay down his life for an estranged and, in the end, murderously hostile people? What of the 'unheard' prayer in Gethsemane: 'My Father if it be possible, let this cup pass from me ...' (Mt 26: 39); and the cry of 'despair' on Calvary: 'My God, my God, why hast thou forsaken me?' (Mt 27:46)

The depth of Jesus' suffering, physical, mental and spiritual, is clearly gospel truth. His conviction of mission given by Abba, Father, and his energetic pursuit of it had led, as he increasingly anticipated, to his suffering and dying for friend and enemy. Passion for the Kingdom, for the will of the Father and the liberation of humanity had brought him all this way for birth and death. In his most abandoned moments he could add to his prayer in the garden, 'nevertheless not as I will but as thou wilt,' (Mt 26:39) while Luke records his last words as, 'Father into thy hands I commit my spirit.' (Lk 23:46)

The Christ of Passion is at once the enduring, suffering and sacrificing Christ of the Passion Narratives and the loving, caring and creative Christ of ministry and parable. The passion for people, for justice, for the new fellowship of the Kingdom of God, the passion of Christ's ministry, is expressed in healing, imaginative and creative word. The Christ of Passion is also the Christ of Poetry. In him and through him, the creative Word and Spirit of God enter fully and finally into the passion of humanity in both its suffering and creative moments. The passionate God has become human. 'An immortal passion breathes in human clay.' (W.B. Yeats) And so it remains.

In his 'Ecce Homo', David Gascoyne captures so well the continuing suffering passion of Jesus and of his God.

> Whose is this horrifying face,
> This putrid flesh, discoloured, flayed,
> Fed on by flies, scorched by the sun? ...
> Behold the Man: He is Man's Son ...
> He is in agony till the world's end.
>
> And we must never sleep during that time!
> He is suspended on the cross-tree now
> And we are onlookers at the crime,

Callous contemporaries of the slow
Torture of God ...

Not from a monstrance silver-wrought
But from the tree of human pain
Redeem our sterile misery,
Christ of Revolution and of Poetry,
That man's long journey through the night
May not have been in vain.

Mayo God Help Us
Mayo theology can, at best, be just one more very modest step in the search for God and for some contemporary way of speaking and living God's presence. The passionate power of nature, and humanity's passionate response to it, has entered deeply into the shaping of Mayo and its people. It inevitably affects their search in faith. For them God's power and presence cannot be separated from wind and sea and hungry grass. The passion of creation signals something of the passion of Creator. In personal passion the biblical writers, and their mystical and saintly successors, have not flinched at comparing God's love for people and person with the most intense erotic human passion. A great love-poem like *Úna Bhán*, from that disputed border country between Mayo and Roscommon near Ballaghadereen, connects with so much other love-literature in opening us up to the depth and intensity of the human loving which at its best reflects divine love.

Passion for people, in humans and in God, transcends sexual passionate love and any immediate beloved. A just society requires and frequently receives commitment of equal conviction and energy. God's quest for justice on earth through Israel prompted the prophet Jeremiah's summary of life that to do justice is to know God. (Jer 22:15-16) That God and that God's justice still constitute the central task of Mayo, and all theologians.

The Christ of Passion and of Poetry has his particular Mayo appeal. The movement and energy released in the world by the impact of this passion-filled figure, offer the surest way into the movement and energy that is God's very self. The passion of God, as expressed in the creation and salvation of the world, emerges in the story of Christ as the story of the powerful and intimate relationships of Father, Son and Holy Spirit. What some early Eastern theologians described as the dynamic dance within God (*periochoresis*) exposes the internal and interpersonal passion of the God who is finally and supremely described as love in the New Testament. (1 Jn 4:8) Further exploration of God as vital communion, with all the implications for God as passionate, will have to await a second Mayo book of theology.

Such exploration would in any case be impertinent; all theology finally is; Mayo theology no less and no more than any other kind. The historical inferiority attributed to (or imagined by) Mayo people may provide a useful safeguard here. Despite the divine summons and human need to use our minds and our language in the search for God, we have to remember the limitations of human mind and language faced with the ultimate and the divine. For all theology analogy rules OK. So we may properly say of any universal or particular theology what we say of our own: Mayo theology, God help us.

The Contributors

JOSEPH CASSIDY was born and reared in Charlestown. Ordained priest for the Diocese of Achonry, he is now Archbishop of Tuam.

ENDA McDONAGH was born and grew up in Bekan. He is a priest of the Archdiocese of Tuam and Professor of Moral Theology at St Patrick's College, Maynooth.

SEÁN FREYNE was born in Kilkelly and grew up in Tooreen. He is Professor of Theology at Trinity College, Dublin.

MICHAEL NEARY was born and grew up in Castlebar. A priest of the Archdiocese of Tuam, he lectures in New Testament at St Patrick's College, Maynooth.

ENDA LYONS is a native of Ballyhaunis, where he grew up. A priest of Tuam Archdiocese, he now works at theology at local level with small groups.

AUGUSTINE VALKENBURG, a Dominican Priest from Ballinrobe, died unexpectedly shortly before the publication of this book. Ar dheis Dé go raibh a anam.

LEON Ó MÓRCHÁIN, a native of Louisburgh, is a priest of the Diocese of Galway, where he is Parish Priest in Barna. Founder Editor of the Lousiburgh parish magazine, *An Choinneal*.

DONAL DORR is from Foxford. A Kiltegan priest and theologian, he works in Ireland and in the Third World.

MARY GUY was born and grew up in Ballina. An Ursuline Sister, she took a master's degree in theology in Cambridge, Mass., and now works as a Spiritual Director in Ireland and abroad.

BRENDAN HOBAN was born in Ballycastle. A priest of the Diocese of Killala, he is now Director of Communications for the diocese.

BEN KIMMERLING lived in England when first married. Then she, her husband and family settled in Pontoon – near her native Foxford. She is involved in church renewal.

NED CROSBY was born and reared in Ballinrobe. A priest of Galway Diocese, he is chaplain to the travellers there.

THOMAS WALDRON is a native of Castlebar. He is a priest of the Archdiocese of Tuam and works in Claremorris, Co Mayo.

JOHN F DEANE was born in Achill Island. Poet and poetry publisher, founder of *Poetry Ireland*, his collection *The Stylised City* appears in 1990.

PATRICK O BRIEN was born in Claremorris. As a priest of the Tuam Archdiocese, he has worked on Clare Island-Inishturk and Skehana, East Galway. His first collection of poetry, *A Book of Genesis*, was published in 1988.

PÁDRAIG STANDÚN was born and reared at Ballydavock, Belcarra. A priest of the Archdiocese of Tuam, he is curate in Inis Meáin, having served previously in Inis Oirr and An Cheathrú Rua.